FROM DREAMS TO VENTURES, 10 LATINA
ENTREPRENEURS LEADING THE WAY.

BREAKING THE GLASS CEILING

LATINA ENTREPRENEUR

HANNA OLIVAS AND ADRIANA LUNA CARLOS
ALONG WITH 8 POWERFUL LATINA ENTREPRENEURS

ISBN: 978-1-966798-26-2

TABLE OF CONTENTS

INTRODUCTION

In a world where leadership has long been dominated by a select few, *Breaking the Glass Ceiling: Latina Entrepreneur* offers a powerful and inspiring lens through which to view the resilience, strength, and innovation of Latina women in business. This book is more than just a collection of stories; it's a celebration of how these incredible women have defied odds, challenged stereotypes, and redefined what it means to be a leader in the entrepreneurial space.

Within these pages, you'll meet Latina entrepreneurs from a wide spectrum of industries—each with her own unique story of struggle, perseverance, and triumph. These women are not only breaking barriers but also creating pathways for the next generation of Latina leaders. Their journeys are marked by determination, passion, and a commitment to cultural pride, proving that success in entrepreneurship isn't defined by one's background, but by the strength of one's vision and resolve.

Through candid interviews, personal anecdotes, and insightful reflections, *Breaking the Glass Ceiling: Latina Entrepreneur* provides readers with an intimate look into the challenges faced by Latina entrepreneurs—challenges that often arise from both gender and cultural expectations—and the strategies they've employed to overcome them. From navigating the delicate balance between tradition and progress to leveraging cultural identity as a source of power, these women have shown the world that their voices are invaluable, their impact undeniable, and their leadership transformative.

This book is not just a narrative of struggle but a beacon of empowerment and inspiration. It challenges all readers—whether entrepreneurs themselves, aspiring business leaders, or those passionate about diversity and inclusion—to rethink the boundaries of success and leadership. The

Latina entrepreneurs featured here exemplify the limitless potential that exists when talent, tenacity, and a deep connection to one's roots converge.

Join us in celebrating these extraordinary women, their groundbreaking achievements, and their undeniable contributions to the future of entrepreneurship. *Breaking the Glass Ceiling: Latina Entrepreneur* is a testament to the fact that the sky is not the limit for Latina entrepreneurs—it's just the beginning.

Hanna Olivas

Founder and CEO of SHE RISES STUDIOS

https://www.linkedin.com/company/she-rises-studios/
https://www.facebook.com/sherisesstudios
https://www.instagram.com/sherisesstudios_llc/
www.SheRisesStudios.com

Author, Speaker, and Founder. Hanna was born and raised in Las Vegas, Nevada, and has paved her way to becoming one of the most influential women of 2022. Hanna is the co-founder of She Rises Studios and the founder of the Brave & Beautiful Blood Cancer Foundation. Her journey started in 2017 when she was first diagnosed with Multiple Myeloma, an incurable blood cancer. Now more than ever, her focus is to empower other women to become leaders because The Future is Female. She is currently traveling and speaking publicly to women to educate them on entrepreneurship, leadership, and owning the female power within.

Breaking the Glass Ceiling: A Latina Entrepreneur's Journey

By Hanna Olivas

As a Latina entrepreneur, my path has been one of pride, struggle, and triumph. I stand today as a woman who has not only broken barriers but also defied the expectations that society, culture, and even my own circumstances placed on me. My journey toward success as a Latina entrepreneur is deeply personal, but it also represents the collective experience of many women like me who have had to carve out spaces where none existed. This chapter isn't just about my success; it's about a movement of Latinas pushing through the ceilings that have tried to keep us down.

What makes my journey even more profound is that, though my heritage comes from my father's side, he wasn't the one who helped me embrace my Latina roots. My father walked out when I was young, leaving my mother and grandmother to raise me. My mother and grandmother, neither of whom are Latina, could have chosen to let me disconnect from that part of myself, but they didn't. Instead, they taught me to embrace my heritage fully, to take pride in the beauty of my culture, and to never forget where I came from. It's one of the greatest gifts they could have given me.

"You're more than the circumstances you were born into; you're a product of how you choose to rise above them." That's something I've learned throughout my life. My mom and grandmother, though not Latina, understood the power and significance of culture. They made sure I was connected to my roots, that I embraced the traditions, the language, and the beauty of being Latina. And because of that, I carry my heritage with pride in everything I do. They weren't just raising me to be successful; they were raising me to be proud of every piece of who I am.

Being raised in a household where my Latina heritage was celebrated rather than neglected was powerful. It was a reminder that, even though my father wasn't present, my identity wasn't lost. My culture is a part of me, and it always will be. This pride in my roots has fueled much of my success because "knowing where you come from gives you the strength to go wherever you want."

But as proud as I am of my culture, being a Latina entrepreneur hasn't been easy. The world doesn't always open doors for women like me, especially not in the business world. Latinas are often seen as "less than," and the stereotypes that follow us can be suffocating. We are expected to be humble, to stay quiet, to not take up too much space. We are expected to fit into roles that are comfortable for others but confining for us. But as a proud Latina entrepreneur, I refuse to be boxed in by those expectations.

"Breaking the glass ceiling isn't just about breaking through for yourself; it's about breaking through for those who come after you." Every barrier I've broken, every space I've walked into where I wasn't expected to be, has been about more than just me. It's been about paving the way for other Latinas, for the young girls who are told that their dreams are too big, too ambitious. It's about showing them that not only can they reach for the stars, but they can also shatter the ceilings above them.

There's a unique strength that comes from being Latina, a resilience that has been passed down through generations. Even though my father wasn't there to teach me about our heritage, the stories of my ancestors still live within me. Latinas have always been fighters—strong, capable, and unstoppable. We carry the weight of our families, our communities, and our dreams on our shoulders, and yet we continue to rise. "Ser Latina es ser fuerte, valiente, y capaz de lograr todo lo que soñamos." (Being Latina is being strong, brave, and capable of achieving everything we dream of.) That is the essence of who we are.

For me, breaking the glass ceiling wasn't just about proving that I could succeed in a world that wasn't built for me. It was about embracing every aspect of my Latina identity and using it to fuel my success. Our culture is rich in tradition, passion, and creativity. We bring something unique to the table, and for too long, that has been overlooked. But I'm here to remind the world that "our culture is not a barrier; it is our greatest strength."

One of the most difficult things I've had to navigate as a Latina entrepreneur is the way we are often underestimated. I've walked into boardrooms where people didn't expect me to be in charge. I've pitched ideas to rooms full of people who didn't think I had the expertise or the vision to lead. I've been asked questions that wouldn't be asked of my male or non-Latina counterparts. But every time I've felt that doubt from others, I've turned inward, reminding myself of this truth: "I don't need anyone else's validation to know my worth. I define my success."

There's something incredibly powerful about being the unexpected success story. Latinas are often seen as caretakers, service workers, or background players. While there is nothing wrong with these roles— they are honorable—they are not the only roles we can play. We are leaders. We are visionaries. We are innovators. And when I walk into those rooms where I'm not expected to thrive, I carry my culture with me like armor. "Being Latina means leading with both strength and grace. It means breaking down doors not just for yourself, but for everyone who comes after you."

In my early days as an entrepreneur, I often found myself trying to fit into the mold of what I thought a "successful" businesswoman should look like. I tried to tone down my culture, to fit into the boxes that others wanted to place me in. But the more I tried to fit in, the more I realized that I was dimming my light. The success I was seeking couldn't be found by conforming to others' expectations. "Success doesn't come from fitting in; it comes from standing out." And standing out meant embracing every part of who I am, including my Latina heritage.

When I finally let go of the need to fit in and fully embraced my identity, everything changed. I stopped apologizing for my culture, my accent, my background. I started celebrating it. I realized that my Latina identity was not something to be hidden or toned down—it was my superpower. It's what makes me unique in a world that tries to make everyone the same. And I'm proud of that. "Being Latina is my power, and I will never shrink myself to make others comfortable."

But breaking the glass ceiling as a Latina entrepreneur isn't just about overcoming external challenges. It's also about overcoming the internal barriers we carry. The doubts, the insecurities, the fear of not being good enough. These are things I've had to wrestle with time and time again. Society tells us that as Latinas, we are not enough—that we don't belong in spaces of power, that we are too much or not enough all at once. But every time I've faced those doubts, I've reminded myself of something powerful: "I am enough, just as I am. I am worthy of every success that comes my way."

As Latinas, we carry the weight of our ancestors' struggles, the hopes of our families, and the expectations of our communities. We are expected to succeed not just for ourselves, but for those who came before us and those who will come after us. And that responsibility is both a blessing and a burden. But it's a burden I carry with pride because I know that every step I take, every success I achieve, is one more step toward making it easier for the next generation of Latina entrepreneurs.

When I think about what it means to break the glass ceiling as a Latina entrepreneur, I think about legacy. I think about the women who will follow in my footsteps, who will look to my story and see what is possible. "My success is not just for me; it's for every Latina who dreams of something bigger." I want to be remembered not just for my achievements, but for the impact I made on my community, for the doors I opened, for the ceilings I shattered.

My journey as a Latina entrepreneur has been filled with both laughter and tears. There have been moments of immense joy and pride, as well as moments of deep frustration and doubt. But through it all, I have remained grounded in my faith, my culture, and my belief in myself. "Faith has been my anchor through the storms, and my culture has been the wind beneath my wings." Without these two guiding forces, I don't know where I would be.

One of the most important things I've learned on this journey is the power of community. As Latinas, we are not alone in our struggles. We come from a lineage of women who have fought, survived, and thrived despite the odds. And when we come together, when we support one another, there is nothing we cannot achieve. "Together, we rise." That's the mantra I live by. And that's what I want every Latina to know—you don't have to do it alone. There is a community of women who will lift you, support you, and cheer you on every step of the way.

As I look back on my journey and reflect on all that I've accomplished, I am filled with gratitude. Gratitude for my mother and grandmother, who taught me to embrace my Latina heritage even when my father wasn't there. Gratitude for the women who came before me, who fought battles much harder than mine so that I could stand where I am today. And gratitude for the opportunities I've had to break through barriers and create spaces for other Latinas to thrive.

"Breaking the glass ceiling is not a destination; it's a journey." It's about constantly pushing the boundaries of what's possible, not just for ourselves, but for every Latina who dares to dream. It's about creating a world where young Latinas don't have to fight so hard to be seen, heard, and valued. It's about ensuring that the generations who come after us have a smoother path to walk, a higher ceiling to shatter, and more opportunities to thrive.

I want every Latina reading this to know that your dreams are valid. Your voice matters. You are powerful beyond measure. And though the journey may be tough, you are not alone. We are a community, and together, we will continue to rise. "Si se puede." Yes, we can.

So here's to every Latina entrepreneur out there. Here's to the dreams you're building, the barriers you're breaking, and the future you're creating. May you continue to rise, to shatter ceilings, and to inspire the next generation of Latinas to do the same. The world is ready for your brilliance, your passion, and your power.

We are Latinas. We are unstoppable.

Adriana Luna Carlos

Founder and CEO of SHE RISES STUDIOS & FENIX TV

https://www.linkedin.com/in/adriana-luna-carlos/
https://www.facebook.com/adrianalunacarlos
https://www.instagram.com/sherisesstudios_llc/
https://www.sherisesstudios.com/
https://fenixtv.app/

Adriana Luna Carlos is an accomplished web and graphic designer, author, and mentor with a passion for helping women succeed in life and business. With over 10 years of experience in graphic and web arts, Adriana has built a reputation as an innovative leader and entrepreneur. In 2020, she co-founded She Rises Studios, a multi-digital media company and publishing house that has helped countless clients achieve their branding and marketing goals. In 2023, she co-created FENIX TV, an online streaming platform that showcases stories of people breaking barriers, shattering stereotypes, and triumphing against the odds.

As an advocate for women's success, Adriana challenges her clients and mentees to strive for nothing less than excellence. She has a deep understanding of the insecurities and challenges that women often face in the business world and provides the guidance and resources needed to overcome them. Her success as a business leader and entrepreneur has made her a sought-after mentor and speaker at events around the world.

Through her work, Adriana has demonstrated a commitment to creating opportunities for women to succeed in business and life. Her passion for innovation, leadership, and women's empowerment has made her a respected figure in the business community, and her impact will undoubtedly continue to inspire and empower women for years to come.

Breaking the Glass Ceiling: My Journey as a Latina Entrepreneur

By Adriana Luna Carlos

Designing My Destiny

From a young age, I was told that I was "lucky." People would marvel at how opportunities seemed to fall into my lap, how success appeared effortless. But what they didn't see were the late nights, the struggles, and the sheer determination that fueled my journey. It wasn't luck—it was resilience, hard work, and an unwavering belief in my own worth.

As an entrepreneur, I've faced my share of obstacles. Society had its own labels for me—too young, too inexperienced, not educated enough. But I knew that my identity was not a limitation; it was my strength. My heritage instilled in me the values of perseverance, community, and innovation. These were the tools I used to carve my own path, to rise above the limitations others tried to place on me.

Finding My Identity in Business

Growing up in a Mexican household while also carrying Italian, Dutch, and Norwegian roots, I always felt like I was navigating between cultures. My family lovingly called me "Güerita," a term of endearment but also a reminder that I looked different. While I was raised fully immersed in Mexican traditions, speaking the language, and living the culture, I sometimes felt that the outside world didn't see me as Latina. But inside, I knew exactly who I was—I was proud of every part of me, and I refused to let others dictate my identity.

This experience shaped how I approached business. I knew what it felt like to not fit into one clear box, and that became my advantage. It allowed me to see things differently, to approach challenges with adaptability, and to create my own lane instead of trying to fit into one that wasn't built for me. I learned that identity is not about how others perceive you—it's about how you define yourself and what you bring to the table.

The Power of Knowing My Worth

One of the greatest challenges women face—especially those who feel caught between cultures—is recognizing and asserting our worth. We are raised to be humble, to serve, to put others first. While those values are beautiful, they can sometimes hold us back from stepping into our full power. I had to unlearn the idea that my value was tied to external validation. Instead, I learned to measure my worth by my own standards—by my skills, my knowledge, and the impact I was making.

When I first started my business, I struggled with pricing my services. I feared that asking for what I deserved would drive clients away. But I soon realized that undervaluing myself didn't just hurt me—it hurt the people who depended on my success. I had to learn to set boundaries, to demand respect, and to recognize that my contributions were just as valuable as anyone else's in the room.

Turning Challenges into Opportunities

Entrepreneurship is not for the faint of heart. The road is paved with uncertainty, failure, and self-doubt. But each challenge carries an opportunity—a lesson that can propel us forward. When I faced skepticism about my abilities, I let my work speak louder than words. When I lacked resources, I found creative ways to make things happen. When doors were closed in my face, I built my own table.

One of the biggest lessons I've learned is that success is not a straight path. It's a winding road filled with detours, setbacks, and breakthroughs. Every challenge I've faced has taught me something invaluable—how to adapt, how to lead, and most importantly, how to believe in myself even when no one else does.

Scaling and Innovation: A Unique Perspective

Entrepreneurs who have grown up navigating multiple cultural identities bring something special to the table—an ability to innovate under pressure, to turn limited resources into thriving businesses, and to lead with heart. Scaling a business requires strategy, but it also requires courage. We must be willing to take risks, to invest in ourselves, and to embrace change.

For me, scaling wasn't just about growing my business—it was about expanding my impact. It was about creating opportunities for other women who, like me, were ready to break barriers. It meant mentoring others, sharing my knowledge, and proving that we belong in every industry, in every boardroom, in every leadership position.

Resilience and Redefining Success

Resilience is not just a skill; it's a survival mechanism. There were moments when I questioned everything—whether I was good enough, whether I was making the right choices, whether I was capable of handling the pressures of running a business. But every doubt became fuel for my determination.

Success is not a single destination; it's an evolving journey. I've learned to redefine success on my own terms. For me, success is about creating opportunities for others, about building something that lasts, about inspiring the next generation of entrepreneurs to dream bigger than ever before.

I have also learned that setbacks are not failures. They are lessons in disguise, guiding us toward a better version of ourselves. Each "no" I received, each challenge I faced, shaped me into a stronger, more determined entrepreneur. I refused to let societal expectations define my potential. Instead, I focused on my vision, my passion, and my ability to create something meaningful.

The Importance of Representation

One of the reasons I am so passionate about my journey as an entrepreneur is because representation matters. When young women see leaders who reflect their own backgrounds—whether fully embraced by one culture or bridging multiple identities—they start to believe that they, too, can achieve greatness.

For far too long, women like me have been underrepresented in the business world. We have been overlooked, underestimated, and undervalued. But that is changing. More of us are stepping into leadership roles, creating our own businesses, and proving that we are a force to be reckoned with.

I want to be part of that movement. I want to show other entrepreneurs that their dreams are valid, that their voices matter, and that their success is possible. The more we uplift each other, the stronger we become as a community.

Daring to Dream Big

Our dreams are not just fantasies—they are blueprints for what's possible. I believe in the power of dreaming big, of envisioning a future where diverse entrepreneurs are celebrated, supported, and empowered.

My journey has taught me that success is not about waiting for the right moment—it's about creating it. It's about believing in yourself so fiercely that no obstacle can shake you. It's about lifting others as you rise because true success is not just personal—it's collective.

To every entrepreneur reading this: You are powerful beyond measure. Your voice matters. Your dreams are valid. Break through the glass ceilings placed before you and show the world what we are capable of. The future belongs to those who dare to dream—and I dare you to dream bigger than ever before.

Leaving a Legacy

As I continue my journey, my ultimate goal is to leave a lasting legacy. I don't just want to build a successful business; I want to create something that will continue to inspire and empower others long after I'm gone. I want to pave the way for future entrepreneurs, to create a world where our voices are heard, our contributions are recognized, and our dreams are limitless.

This journey has not been easy, but it has been worth every challenge. I hope my story serves as a reminder that we are capable of greatness. We are not defined by our struggles but by how we rise above them. We are not limited by society's expectations but by how boldly we choose to defy them.

So to every entrepreneur out there—keep pushing, keep striving, and keep breaking those glass ceilings.

Your Success Action Plan

Here are some steps to help you move forward in your entrepreneurial journey. Use this as a guide to keep yourself accountable, motivated, and constantly growing.

1. **Define Your Vision:** Write down your biggest dream for your business. Be specific and bold.

2. **Identify Three Strengths:** What makes you unique? What skills or qualities set you apart?

3. **Set SMART Goals:** Define goals that are Specific, Measurable, Achievable, Relevant, and Time-bound.

4. **Network with Intention:** Reach out to three people this month who inspire you or who you can collaborate with.

5. **Embrace a Growth Mindset:** Remind yourself that failure is just feedback. Learn, adjust, and keep moving forward.

6. **Prioritize Self-Care:** Your success depends on your well-being. Schedule time for rest and activities that recharge you.

7. **Celebrate Your Wins:** No matter how small, acknowledge your progress. Confidence is built through recognizing achievements.

Mantras for Empowerment

Repeat these affirmations daily to strengthen your mindset and remind yourself of your power:

- *I am worthy of success and abundance.*
- *My voice and my story matter.*
- *Challenges are stepping stones to my greatest achievements.*
- *I have everything within me to succeed.*
- *I embrace my unique identity and use it to my advantage.*
- *I am creating a legacy of empowerment and inspiration.*

Your journey is just beginning, and the world is waiting to see what you will achieve next.

Ana Martinez, RN

All Travel Worldwide LLC
Travel Advisor

https://www.linkedin.com/in/anamlv
https://www.facebook.com/atwcp
https://www.instagram.com/magicalmomentsnow
https://www.alltravelworldwide.com
https://linktr.ee/magicalmomentsnow

Ana is a homeschooling mom of three beautiful daughters and a versatile professional. As a Registered Nurse, Certified Lactation Counselor, Cruise Planners Travel Advisor, HowMoneyWorks Financial Educator, and author, she has built a diverse career. Ana graduated from the University of Nevada, Las Vegas, in 2013 with a Bachelor of Science in Nursing, gaining experience in various specialties, including labor, delivery, postpartum, and hospice care.

In 2017, she expanded her role as a Certified Lactation Counselor, and in 2022, driven by her passion for travel, she became a Travel Advisor. By 2024, Ana embraced entrepreneurship in the financial industry and began her writing journey, while continuing her previous work.

In her free time, Ana enjoys dancing and traveling fulltime with her family in an RV. She believes life is too short to settle for anything less than extraordinary, especially when it comes to living authentically as your true self

So You Want to Be an Entrepreneur—What's Your Why, and Do You Have What It Takes?

By Ana Martinez, RN

Becoming an entrepreneur is a bold and transformative choice—especially as a Latina entrepreneur—because it requires embracing both the challenges and the unique strengths that come with navigating a path that is often underrepresented yet filled with immense opportunity. It's an exciting journey, but let's be honest—it can also feel overwhelming. Maybe you're wondering if you have what it takes or if you're making the right choice. Let me assure you: You do, and you are. However, timing is crucial. Entrepreneurship isn't just a career choice; it's a mindset and a lifestyle. My goal in this chapter is to replace any fear or doubt you might have with confidence and to provide practical tips to help you thrive on this path.

To begin, entrepreneurship isn't about being fearless; it's about feeling the fear and moving forward anyway. It's about recognizing that you don't need to have all the answers right now. Whether you're just starting out or already navigating the journey, the first and most important question to ask yourself is: Why?

Your why is important as it isn't just your starting point—it's your anchor, it will be the force that will inspire you to take risks, persevere through challenges, and build something truly meaningful. So, dig deep: What gives you the courage to take the next step, even when the whole staircase isn't visible? What fuels your passion and keeps you moving forward even when the road gets tough?

Because let's face it—the road will be tough. Will you have the self-discipline and confidence to keep going? For a long time, you'll face challenges that might make you question everything. You'll want to quit a dozen times—or more—before you know for sure that this is the path you're meant to take. But here's the truth: Those moments of doubt and struggle are part of the process. With the right mindset and tools, you'll find the strength to keep going and build something extraordinary.

As a Latina entrepreneur, my journey was slow and unconventional. Like many Latino families, mine believed that the only path to success was through college and obtaining a degree. For the first part of my life, that's exactly what I pursued. After graduating from high school, I attended the University of Nevada, Las Vegas, where I earned my Bachelor of Science in Nursing. It was a practical degree—one that promised stability—but it wasn't something I was truly passionate about.

I built a stable career, exploring various specialties, from labor and delivery to hospice care. While I found joy in helping patients at their bedside, I never felt truly fulfilled. Over time, the challenges of nursing began to weigh heavily on me. Management pressures, unsafe patient-to-nurse ratios, and the emotional, mental, and physical toll of the work made it increasingly difficult to see a future where I could protect both my license and my well-being.

After my mother died from cancer and spent her last days in a hospital and hours in hospice care, the constant emotional and mental triggers became too much to bear. That loss not only deepened my grief but also made me question whether I was truly living a life aligned with my purpose.

Meanwhile, my partner was already an entrepreneur who had laid a solid foundation for his pool maintenance and repair business. He secured an EIN, obtained a business license with the state and city, opened a business checking account, had insurance, and used QuickBooks for accounting. Through him, I witnessed—and was actively involved in—the trials and tribulations of running a business.

Balancing work and life was no easy feat, especially after we had our daughters. We made plenty of mistakes along the way but gained valuable lessons through challenges like hiring contractors, deciding to accept card payments despite the fees, and experimenting with different business ventures. On a positive note, we found an excellent CPA to manage our bookkeeping and taxes, and we streamlined operations by setting up auto-pay systems.

Thus, as I stated before, entrepreneurship isn't just a career choice; it's a mindset and a lifestyle. While it's not inherently better than other paths, it does require a unique set of qualities, traits, and skills that you can develop over time. In my opinion, the top five areas essential for thriving as an entrepreneur are:

1. **Self-discipline** to creatively stay focused and consistently work toward your goals, finding new ways to stay organized and productive while maintaining focus on what matters most.

2. **Confidence and Grit** to believe in your vision and creatively fuel that vision, while grit ensures you stay confident, even when facing obstacles

3. A willingness to be **coachable** and learn from others, creatively applying what you learn in unique ways.

4. A deep desire to **help people** creatively enables you to approach problem-solving with fresh ideas.

5. **The determination to compete**—not against others, but with the version of yourself you were yesterday.

These qualities, when combined, create the foundation for entrepreneurial success. You don't need to be perfect to start. You just need to start. With the right mindset, support, and tools, you can create the business and life you've always dreamed of. So, are you ready to embrace the journey?

Let's turn your fears into fuel and take that first step toward entrepreneurial success—together. Let's dive into the five areas that drive successful entrepreneurs!

Self-Discipline

Pro: Freedom to work when you want and be present for your family

Con: Laziness/chaos if nothing gets done

Let's start with a few reflection questions:

- Do you make your bed every morning?
- Do you keep your car clean?
- Do you exercise and eat healthy?

These are all things that no one else can make you do. As adults, it's our responsibility to practice self-discipline and take ownership of our actions. Without self-discipline, nothing gets done. As a mother, this quality becomes even more challenging, as motherhood adds its own layer of complexity. Finding ways to complete tasks both personally and professionally requires creativity and support from a village. In my work, *Healthy Glow*, I explore the importance of taking responsibility for your choices and the value of finding your village. Failure to prepare is preparing to fail.

As you step into entrepreneurship, this same principle applies. The majority of people need someone, like a boss, to tell them when to come into work, when to take lunch, and when they can take time off. If that's you, that's okay—it simply means you may not be ready yet to take on the full responsibilities of entrepreneurship, which requires wearing many hats. Alternatively, you may need to start part-time until the habit becomes second nature. Each role is essential to the success of your business, and balancing them effectively is key. Here are the four primary hats you'll need to master over time:

1. **Marketer**—You're responsible for spreading the word about your business, building brand awareness, and attracting customers. In the beginning, you will spend the majority of your time and efforts in this area.

2. **Salesperson**—Closing deals, building relationships, and converting prospects into paying customers is a critical part of your role.

3. **Advisor**—Whether it's guiding your team, offering solutions to clients, or making strategic decisions, you must be a trusted source of insight and expertise in your trade.

4. **Entrepreneur**—You oversee operations and finances, and ensure your business runs smoothly and sustainably.

Confidence and Grit

Pro: Empowerment and growth without limits

Con: Difficulty with rejection, thus unable to be an effective entrepreneur

As humans, we all have insecurities—some more than others. And that's okay. If you find that your insecurities hold you back, it may be a sign that you need time to heal first. Confidence isn't about being perfect; it's about embracing who you are, flaws and all. When you're confident, you're not afraid to talk to people, network, or step out of your comfort zone.

Many people fear rejection, which can stop them from even asking for what they want or need. But with confidence, you can overcome that fear and take action, even when the outcome is uncertain. Confidence allows you to move forward despite the risk of rejection, which is an essential trait for any entrepreneur. Without it, you may find yourself stuck, unable to take the necessary steps to grow your business.

In my works *100 Voices of Women* and *Sensual Symphony*, I explore how living your best life and reclaiming your sensuality both require confidence. It's a quality that comes from within—mentally, emotionally, spiritually, and lastly physically. When you nurture your confidence, you empower yourself to embrace opportunities and challenges with courage. As women, many become mothers, and it will take creativity and grit to stay on this path despite the many interruptions our children will make, how we feel postpartum, and the type of support we receive.

In the end, entrepreneurship is a numbers game. The more people who know you exist, the greater your chances of connecting with those who already want or need your service or product. If you consistently reach out to 15 new people each week and secure at least 5 fact-finding appointments, you should be able to generate business.

For at least the first two years, your focus will be on prospecting and building relationships, with the goal of eventually having people seek you out. During this time, it's important to evaluate your progress regularly. Ask yourself: *Is the phone ringing?*

- If it's not, you have a marketing problem and you need to pick up the phone and call your leads.
- If it is, but you're not closing deals, you have a sales problem.

By identifying and addressing these issues early, you can refine your approach and set yourself up for long-term success.

Coachable

Pro: Access to guidance and proven strategies

Con: Requires humility and willingness to accept feedback

As an entrepreneur, there's no need to reinvent the wheel. Seek help. More importantly, seek a coach or mentor. When you're new to entrepreneurship and business ownership, it can feel overwhelming. The learning curve is steep, and having someone to guide you can make all the difference. In the beginning, it may be hard to accept that:

1. It takes money to make money.
2. Time is infinitely greater than money.

By hiring a coach, you're investing in awareness and significantly reducing your struggles. As a Latina entrepreneur, it was particularly challenging for me, as no one in my family or friend circle had experience in entrepreneurship. Asking for help wasn't easy, but it was necessary.

For years, I would buy a domain on GoDaddy and attempt to manage my own website. Truthfully, I had no idea what I was doing. It wasn't until I finally hired a website designer that things started to take shape. However, one of the best decisions I made was hiring a marketing coach. We met at NurseCon Orlando, and what a blessing it was to connect with her. After years of struggling on my own, I finally had someone who provided a clear roadmap and helped me build a solid foundation for my business.

Between the marketing coach and the website designer, they worked hand in hand to update my website. The result was a site that clearly communicated what I do and made it easy for clients to understand how I can help them. I also learned an important lesson: copywriting wasn't the website designer's strength—they simply followed my instructions, which highlighted the value of expert guidance in every area of business.

Thus, being coachable means being open to learning, accepting feedback, and creatively implementing the strategies of those who've already walked the path. It's one of the smartest investments you can make in yourself and your business, as it allows you to build on the experiences of others and avoid unnecessary mistakes.

Foundation Steps for Starting Your Business (in no particular order):

Set Up a Credit Card Platform

Use a platform like Stripe to handle payments securely and efficiently, making transactions seamless for you and your clients.

Create a Sales Deck

Learn the art of creating compelling offers (Myron Golden's strategies and *$100M Offers* by Alex Hormozi are great resources). Your sales deck should clearly outline your value proposition and solutions.

Choose a Scheduling Tool

Decide between platforms like TidyCal or Calendly to streamline appointment scheduling.

Set Parameters That Fit Your Life

As a mother of three and a partner with a busy schedule, I learned to set appointments at least three days out. This gave me time to arrange childcare or notify my partner so I could focus on my appointments without distractions.

Add a Questionnaire to Appointments

Use a pre-appointment questionnaire to gather important details and set the tone for your meeting.

Create an Electronic Business Card

Platforms like HiHello make it easy to share your contact information professionally and efficiently.

Set Up Video Meeting Tools

Choose between Zoom or Google Meet for virtual appointments, ensuring your setup is ready to go.

Master Appointment Conduct

Avoid solving the client's problem on the initial call. Focus on understanding their needs instead. Ask clarifying questions to dig deeper into their concerns. Be honest about anything that makes you nervous, such as using new technology. Clients will appreciate your authenticity.

Present Your Offer Clearly

Read your presentation or sales deck aloud for transparency and to ensure the client fully understands. After presenting, ask, "*Which option works best for you?*" Then, stay silent. It's hard, but this pause gives the client time to think and respond.

Handle Discounts Thoughtfully

If a client asks for a discount, decide what works for you. For example, you might offer 10% off if they book on the call. Alternatively, you can confidently state your value and explain why your pricing reflects it.

Ask for a Testimonial

After working with the client, request a testimonial. Social proof is invaluable for building credibility.

Email Lists and Newsletters

Only ask clients to join your email list if you already have a newsletter prepared. Offering to send something and failing to follow through can damage trust. Be prepared to nurture your clients as soon as they opt in by having at least 3 automated email sequences prepared for your client to get to know you every other day and ask open ended questions.

Have a Social Media Presence

It's important to be available across different platforms to connect with leads and clients. You can choose the platforms you're most comfortable working with, but consistency is key—both in how often you post and in maintaining a steady presence. I highly recommend creating a Facebook group where your leads and clients can become part of a community. This helps keep them engaged, builds trust, and positions you as an authority in your field.

Create a Lead Magnet

Think about what your ideal client experiences in their daily life—their thoughts, struggles, and the problem you are trying to solve for them. Ask yourself:

- *What do I do?*
- *Who do I do it for?*
- *What is their biggest pain point?*
- *If I could eliminate X problem, how would their life improve?*

With these answers, you can create a lead magnet that attracts your ideal clients and gets them interested in your offer. Lastly, I also highly recommend reading *$100M Leads* by Alex Hormozi—it's packed with valuable insights on marketing and generating leads for your business.

Helping Others

Pro: Creates a sense of fulfillment and purpose

Con: You may overextend yourself

As an entrepreneur, why do you start a business? It's not easy—especially if you're the first in your family to take this path. You may face rejection and doubts from those closest to you. That's why it's essential to choose a business you love, one driven by creativity and a purpose greater than yourself. When your work positively impacts someone's life, it becomes more than just a job—it becomes a mission. Helping others also strengthens your reputation, builds trust, and creates loyal clients or customers who value what you do. On the hard days, knowing you're making a difference and having the grit to persevere will keep you moving forward. A purpose greater than yourself also helps you avoid tying your identity to any one person or company.

On the other hand, while helping others is deeply rewarding, it's equally important to help yourself by valuing your time, energy, and expertise.

You might find it hard to set boundaries, saying "yes" too often or undervaluing your time and services. This can lead to burnout or financial struggles if you're not careful about balancing generosity with sustainability. As a travel advisor, it took me a few years to feel comfortable charging a planning fee. After many experiences where clients didn't book with me, I often felt used and frustrated—no one wants to work for free.

Eventually, I realized I needed to change our business model. With the guidance of a mentor, a Terms and Conditions attorney, and by obtaining a Florida Seller of Travel license, I made the decision to implement a nonrefundable planning fee. This shift not only protected my time and expertise but also ensured I could provide the best service to committed clients.

Competitive with Oneself

Pro: Opens the door to limitless growth and financial success

Con: Stress, exhaustion, and even losing sight of why you started in the first place

When we talk about being competitive, it's not about comparing yourself to others but about striving to be better than you were yesterday. In cross-country running, it's called a PR—personal record. You're running against yourself, not the other racers. Personal growth in entrepreneurship works the same way. Looking back at others only slows you down and distracts you from the path ahead. By focusing on improving your personal performance and meeting your goals, you set the stage for long-term wealth and fulfillment. This mindset keeps you motivated, forward-thinking, creative, and adaptable, ensuring you're always moving toward bigger opportunities. Self-reflection and balance are key. Take time to celebrate your wins—big or small—and keep moving forward with compassion and empathy for yourself. Only you know your circumstances. Only you can define what your ideal work-life balance looks like for yourself and your family because the downside of being highly competitive with yourself is the risk of burnout. When you constantly push for better results without pausing to celebrate your wins, you can become overly critical of your progress.

Conclusion

Becoming a Latina entrepreneur is not just a career path—it's a journey of personal growth, resilience, and self-discovery. Along the way, you'll face challenges, celebrate wins, and learn lessons that will shape both your business and your character. Whether it's building self-discipline, growing your confidence, or staying competitive with yourself, each step you take brings you closer to your goals.

Remember, entrepreneurship is not about perfection. It's about progress. It's about showing up every day with a clear purpose, a strong "why," and the courage to keep moving forward, even when the road gets tough.

You have what it takes to succeed, but success doesn't happen overnight. Build your foundation, stay coachable, and remain focused on helping others. Celebrate your growth and learn from your setbacks. And most importantly, enjoy the process—because the journey is just as important as the destination.

Now, it's your turn. Take that first step, embrace the challenges, and build the life and business you've always dreamed of. **If you need guidance or support along the way, I'm here to help. Reach out, and together, we can create a plan to turn your entrepreneurial dreams into reality**. You've got this, and I'm excited to help you make it happen!

Claudia Noriega-Bernstein

Abundance Coach, Podcast Host & Published Author

https://www.linkedin.com/in/claudia-noriega-bernstein/
https://www.facebook.com/claudianoriegabernstein/
https://www.instagram.com/Claudia_Noriega_Bernstein
https://claudianoriegabernstein.com/

Claudia is an Abundance Coach, mentor, artist, writer, philanthropist, mother, and wife. During her career as a journalist, she has worked for magazines and television in South America and the US, touching subjects from parenting, forgiveness, abundance, how to manifest, and growth to political issues.

As a life/abundance coach, she has helped people, especially women, from different backgrounds, discover and implement the full potential of their own creative powers for personal growth and self-healing.

Her books BRIGHTER DAYS 88 Most important lessons learned in live for women that wants to increase their confidence, resilience and courage; her journals for kids , men and women, as well as a series of children's book to give tools to parents, teachers, and caregivers, on how to speak to children about difficult subjects like, death, divorce and secrets "Valentina and her white Elephant" all available on Amazon and her website.

From Roots to Resilience: A Latina's Journey

By Claudia Noriega-Bernstein

Growing up in South America was probably the best school of life I could have ever asked for because it showed me a reality so different from the one I would face one day in the United States, and that taught me what was probably one of the best tools I still have in my toolbox: resilience.

For Americans, Latins are a homogenous group of people; they perceive us all the same, and they don't even imagine the palette of beautiful colors each of our countries and cultures have. I am very grateful to this country, yet that doesn't blind me from seeing the lack of knowledge some people have about us, our potential, and, more so, the real reason why we ended up sharing this land.

Moving to Florida first and then to Las Vegas wasn't something I planned, but it happened organically, and I took every challenge and every opportunity the same way. I've been in this country for over 32 years yet, funny thing, I am still considered a foreigner.

Arriving in this country in my early twenties, armed with determination and dreams, I soon encountered the harsh reality of societal biases and diminishing perceptions of women, particularly Latinas.

At first, I didn't have any evidence about the way many Americans feel about us, we were lucky to spend a lot of time in Miami, where you can be an American Latino and feel welcome, but not long after being in other states I started to notice different attitudes from people when I would talk to them, and they would hear my accent. It wasn't until one day, while on tour with my husband in St Louis, Missouri, that I really understood how we are perceived.

I had gone to the mall to look for a dress; although I was pregnant with my first daughter, Thalia, I was pretty small, so regular dresses a couple of sizes bigger were still fitting me just fine.

I decided to stop in a store that had this very cute romper displayed in the window. I walked in and asked the lady working there if I could try the dress they had on a mannequin. To my surprise, the sales lady, an American, told me that they didn't have any dresses in my size in the store. Without giving it more thought, I left the store and went to find my husband, who had gone to buy batteries.

After we met, he asked me if I had found the dress I was looking for, so I told him they didn't have my size. He then asked me if there was anything else in the store I liked, and I said, "The lady told me they didn't have anything in my size, she was a little short and matter-of-fact, so I didn't ask anything else."

He then said to me, "Let's go back." I didn't really want to; the lady was not very kind, and I didn't like her energy, and I didn't want to make a big deal, so I stayed outside the store while he went to ask for a different style. The sales lady asked him what size he needed and, to my surprise, proceeded to hand him the romper I had just asked for.

I didn't understand what had just happened, I thought maybe she didn't understand me... Sometimes, we don't think people are capable of doing things that we are not capable of doing, so why would this lady tell me that they didn't have my size when, in fact, she did?

My husband called me to come inside the store to try it on. The sales lady seemed puzzled and a little annoyed. Once I got in the store, my husband asked the lady: Why did you tell my wife that you didn't have her size? And her answer struck me; without hesitation, she said to my husband, "I didn't think she could afford it." I got a taste that day of what it really meant to be discriminated against, how Latinas are perceived in this country, and how some people will treat me differently just because of my accent and looks without knowing anything else about me.

I got so much clarity in that moment that I made a promise to myself: I would never again allow anyone to categorize me based on my accent, where I was from, or the way I looked.

I was no longer going to allow anyone to limit my potential because I was a Latin woman.

You see, when we go through struggles, when we face challenges, those moments, those circumstances are the ones that are going to teach us our biggest lessons. Sometimes, we have to go through the rain before we see the rainbow; sometimes, life will give us the test without giving us time to learn the lesson, and if we only focus on getting to the final line, or the rainbow, we will miss out on the journey itself. The rain is our best teacher! When circumstances challenge us, we have the choice to shrink to fit or to embrace those challenges and grow with them. One of those challenges of moving to this country was the sense of belonging. I didn't feel it for many years, yet that wasn't an unfamiliar feeling for me.

I come from a line of strong, self-sufficient women. I have been influenced by them, and I always knew I was made for more. I had a mother who was ahead of her time when it came to being a businesswoman. In a time when women were expected to stay home and raise kids, my mother never allowed those expectations to hold her back or pin her in a place that she didn't feel comfortable in. She ran restaurants and nightclubs, owned a Travel Agency, and had an import and export company that allowed her to travel the world, among other things. She felt in her element when she traveled. And for many years, I didn't understand why she was absent, yet now, as an adult and with no judgment, I see what she was looking for. It wasn't just the financial independence she wanted for herself but the feeling of accomplishment she was after. The feeling of being enough. I learned that from her.

When my brother was diagnosed with cancer at 19, she moved the family to the United States without hesitation. And she started again from zero, but all those years of traveling and entrepreneurial experience served her to create a new life in this country. That was another nugget I got from that experience. Years later, I followed, and although I didn't have a clear idea about what I wanted to accomplish, I knew I got in me what it would take to succeed and to make a difference.

I am my biggest project, and although my limiting beliefs can and would hold me back if I allow it, I always knew my vision and my purpose would bring me to the place I needed to be to create a life for myself. It wasn't always easy: I faced many obstacles, doors were shut in my face, and I got a lot of NOs, but my vision was clear, my girls were and still are my WHY, and my intention is always my "how," so I evolved as I learned more tools.

I had to have pillars and a structure that would help me give my girls the consistency they needed to feel safe. I must say that keeping my roots and traditions plays an important part in my daughters' upbringing. Not only because growing up in a foreign country sometimes makes you emulate the culture of that country, we all want to feel we belong, but because I didn't want them to become somebody so different from who I am and lose their identity in the process.

There was always Latin music playing in the car and at home, so they would feel the rhythm of our culture in their souls. My kids grew up watching American sitcoms and Latin soap operas, they grew up eating hamburgers and arroz Tapado, which is a typical Peruvian dish. We celebrated holidays and shared traditions, and they were always curious to learn more about my country, which made me very happy. They would laugh when a Spanish friend would come to our home, and they would introduce themselves by Americanized names, and I would ask them what their mother called them because that's how their name should be pronounced. It was always important that my daughters grew up knowing who they were, knowing their worth, and knowing, respecting, and honoring their heritage.

Those things that make us different are the same things that make us unique.

After a few years in Las Vegas, I divorced my husband, and suddenly, I found myself very sick with cancer, divorced, with three kids under five to raise and support and no family or support system in sight; the road ahead seemed daunting. My ex-husband's lack of cooperation at that time only added to the challenges, but again, I refused to be defined by circumstance. In those early years, survival meant creativity and resourcefulness.

The first years were tough: selling my belongings became a temporary solution to meet ends, but it was clear that I needed more sustainable options. Juggling multiple jobs, including working at a daycare to be closer to my youngest daughter Sophia, who wasn't old enough yet to go to Pre-K like her sister Isabella, who was three then, became my reality as I navigated the delicate balance of work and motherhood. Sometimes, I go back to memory lane, and I remember how scared I was yet committed to creating a joyful and sustained life for myself and my girls.

But when they were asleep at night, I would journal and work on ideas for future business. On one of those nights in the quiet of my living room, with my three daughters peacefully sleeping, I found myself grappling with the weight of uncertainty. It was in those moments, among the challenges of single motherhood and the aftermath of divorce, that I embarked on a journey of resilience and reinvention.

Despite the challenges, I remained faithful in my belief that I was destined for more. An opportunity at the Paris Hotel opened doors for me, where my multilingual skills became my greatest asset. I had no idea what my new challenges would involve, but I had a vision, and now I finally had health insurance, too.

Through chance encounters and unexpected connections, I began to explore new avenues. At that time, we were living in an apartment complex close to the kids' school. One day, while picking up my mail, I met my friend Adriene, who was walking her dog, Britt. Adriene was a nurse technician but also a Mary Kay Consultant on the side. She took me to meet her director, and in a week, I was selling Mary Kay door-to-door. This gave me the flexibility to spend time with my kids in the afternoon, they no longer had to stay in Safeky. Yay!

At the Paris Hotel, I met a girl who was working at the Front Desk called Deidra; she, like me, three years ago, was going through a divorce and needed a place to stay. I decided that it was time to move to a house, so I offered to let her to move with us. She did. It was good for my girls and her son Luis, who was the same age as my Sophia. She was a realtor part-time and working with a fabulous lady called Hali who had a group of ladies realtors working for her; so through her, I met many realtors, and I thought of the possibility of working with them. I registered in the Broward Community College to learn how to build websites, and just like that, I created another source of income. At that time, I was working three jobs: Concierge at the Paris Hotel, Mary Kay Consultant in the afternoons, and updating websites for realtors at night for Hali and her Angels, laying the foundation for my entrepreneurial journey.

As I delved into the world of Mary Kay and web design, I realized that these ventures, while fulfilling, were only the beginning. I was determined to create a sustainable income that would afford me more time with my girls.

At the hotel, I was dealing with a lot of high-end guests, better known as VIPs, and I noticed that baskets would be delivered to their rooms prior to arriving, I spoke with a few hostesses and asked them if they would give me the chance to create a couple of baskets for their guests. I already had access to the Mary Kay products at cost, I only needed to find other stuff to put in the baskets to make them attractive. I also contacted my friend John, Seed for us, and asked him if he would buy small baskets or anything from me to give to his clients. Seed was a CPA and Financial Advisor. He said YES! I took a leap of faith and founded Executive Gift Services. He was my first client.

From crafting personalized baskets, or little coffee mugs with a Mary Kay hand cream and a biscotti I called "Thanks a Latte," to cultivating relationships with clients, every step was a testament to my unwavering commitment to success.

My friend Paul had a little casita he wasn't using, so I took the mess that was my living room, I had it filled with baskets, Mary Kay products, coffee mugs, shredded paper, etc., to his casita, which became my headquarters.

The road to entrepreneurship was not without its obstacles. My relationship with Deidra went south as I wasn't fond of some of her choices, so I decided to move to another house. At that time, my finances were in much better shape, so my girls didn't have to share a room anymore. It wasn't easy at first. I faced countless challenges along the way, but I emerged stronger, turning setbacks into stepping stones and adversity into opportunity.

I stopped working for Hali, so now I was able to sleep more than four hours a night. After a few months, I quit my job at the Paris Hotel, and my business became my only source of income. I was no longer doing facials for Mary Kay, yet I was one of the top sellers as I was still buying ridiculous amounts of products for my baskets.

As I reflect on my journey, I am reminded of the power of resilience, determination, and unwavering faith. My story is not just one of personal triumph but a testament to the limitless potential within each of us. As I empower myself, I empower other women to break free from the pressure of societal expectations and chart their own path to success, because it is through our collective strength and determination that we shatter glass ceilings and pave the way for a new era of Latina leadership.

This is the story of how I shattered barriers, defied expectations, and transformed adversity into opportunity. In sharing my story, I hope to inspire women everywhere to embrace their inherent strength, pursue their passions, and defy the odds because when we believe in ourselves and our abilities. There is no limit to what we can achieve as long as we stay true to ourselves, and that is the billboard I want to be for my daughters so although they were born here in the United States and will have incredible opportunities, their identity rests firmly in the fact that they are Latinas like their mother.

Being a Latina is an honor and a privilege. Although sometimes, it could be a challenge because of the dualities of the two worlds we share in this country, there is nothing we cannot accomplish if we have a clear vision, a purpose, and an intention to create a better, more empathetic and inclusive world for our daughters. We are our best asset, let's be proud of our roots and the many colors of our cultures. We are a beautiful quilt, and we can only fly if we embrace each other.

Mercedes Tan

Owner of Minions Construction

https://www.facebook.com/share/18NGse8Xmp/
https://www.instagram.com/mercedes.tan

I'm lifelong resident of Las Vegas. Having grown up in this vibrant and diverse city with an amazing Cuban single mom I have always believed in finding the story and lesson that each person has to offer. Watching my mom work as a porter at the historic Showboat Hotel with a smile for everyone that she came in contact with made me want to have the same love for life that she did. I live by the saying, "in struggle lies evolution," believing that through challenges, we uncover our true strength and potential. Every setback is a lesson, and every triumph is a reminder of the resilience within. So thankful for my daughter and her love and support and cheers to the sisterhood that God has blessed with.

Tangled Roots: A Journey of Resilience, Heritage, and Self-Acceptance

By Mercedes Tan

I always stood out because of my hair. My naturally jet-black ringlets set me apart from my peers, whose "perfect" tresses were uniform, silky, and smooth. Growing up, my relationship with my hair was complicated, to say the least. There were times I resented it, wishing I could blend in. But as I matured, I began to appreciate its wild spirit, its refusal to conform. My hair became a symbol of my journey toward radical self-acceptance. It was my "Mercedes Signature." At one point, I believed many of my opportunities came from the unforgettable impression my hair left. What I once saw as a curse, making me stand out awkwardly, I came to see as a blessing that made me unique. My hair, much like me, was a force to be reckoned with.

It wasn't until later in life that I realized it wasn't just my hair that defined me, but the rich cultural threads woven into my very being by my parents. I am a first-generation Latina-American, born to a Cuban mother and Chinese father.

My mom, Olga, often recounted her stories of growing up in Matanzas and Varadero with a wistful fondness. She painted pictures of long nights dancing on the beach to lively music, the sweet scent of guava in the air, and holidays spent with her loving family. Even as a child, I could sense the bittersweetness in her stories, a nostalgic longing to return to a time she could never relive. Despite this, she always managed to shake off the melancholy and return to her vibrant self.

Mom was exiled from Cuba when she fled the authoritarian Castro regime in 1966. It was a harrowing journey, and she fought tooth and nail to escape. She eventually made her way to Spain, where she met my dad, Sergio. Dad, also from Cuba but of Chinese descent, had fled the country for similar reasons. They married shortly after meeting, driven by a shared dream of a better life. Dad visited America to see if the American Dream was real, sending Mom letters filled with hope and plans for their future family.

They immigrated to America and started their lives in Chicago, where Dad opened a Lechonera that became a beloved lunch spot for many Illinois politicians. I was born during this time. One of my earliest memories is from my fourth birthday when my parents got me a Batman cake. I wasn't particularly into superheroes, but it highlighted how my parents, despite being unfamiliar with American culture, tried their best to make me happy.

We eventually moved to Las Vegas, NV, where my parents' relationship began to fall apart. Mom ended up raising me on her own, working as a porter at the famous Showboat Casino to provide for us. Despite our limited means, she scraped together every penny to send me to First Shepard, a prestigious Lutheran private school. She knew that the other students, their parents, and the teachers could offer me a support network our small family couldn't. At private school, I formed lifelong friendships that I still cherish today, forty years later.

Mom's shifts often extended past the time I was dismissed from school. Some days, I stayed with friends until Mom could pick me up, but other days, I waited at the Showboat until she finished work. I fondly remember sitting in the powder room while Mom's coworkers— waitresses, hostesses, housekeepers—took turns watching over me. They brought me treats like slices of pie from the café. They cared for me because they loved Mom. Despite the language barrier, their affection for her was palpable. Mom spoke only Spanish, while they spoke only English, yet they understood and admired her strength and kindness.

Growing up, I eventually found myself married at 21 to a man who was 46 in Reno. It was a bizarre and ill-fated marriage. He was the VP of food and drink for a casino, and I discovered his infidelity. The divorce was a turning point; I had to rebuild my life from scratch. I became a cocktail waitress, a job I had never imagined doing. I never told Mom about the divorce. When I started waitressing, I stood out to the Carranos, a powerful casino family. It was a humbling and enlightening experience. One of the Carranos offered me a choice: work at the front desk for $9 an hour or cocktail in the pit for $40 an hour. I chose the latter. My left arm became incredibly strong from carrying trays, and people often mistook me for someone else's wife. I proudly corrected them, saying, "No, I'm Mercedes."

I met many wonderful people and had a lot of fun during my time cocktailing. In Reno, I met my daughter's father and became pregnant. I went to the doctor, thinking I had the flu, when they told me, "Congratulations." Confused, I asked why, and that's when the doctor revealed I was pregnant.

The news was shocking, but I embraced my new role as a single mother with determination, just as Mom had done for me. I called Mom, who was still in Las Vegas, and told her I was coming home. She reassured me, saying she would be there for me.

I informed the Carranos I was quitting to return to Las Vegas. I knew Reno didn't offer many opportunities, and I could build a better life for my daughter and me in Las Vegas. The Carranos insisted that's not how things worked, but I stood firm in my decision. They eventually wished me well.

My daughter, Sistina, is my greatest privilege in life, and I was committed to fighting tooth and nail to provide for her, just as Mom had done for me. I began working at AT&T in the early 2000s, where I met Jodi, a woman who would become my mentor. One day, Jodi came into the AT&T store I managed, looking for a new phone. I sold her a Blackberry, which was cutting edge at the time. I was a huge advocate for the Blackberry and had one of the first in town. I told Jodi she could take it on a trial basis. We communicated via email, and she told me she loved the phone. She soon returned and asked for twelve more Blackberries for her team, and I set them all up. That's when Jodi asked if I wanted to stay at AT&T. I replied, "Where else would I go? I'm not looking for another job." She encouraged me to listen to her pitch.

Jodi worked for Pioneer Title, a company that would later become Ticor Title. I knew nothing about the industry, so I asked how many companies in town did title work. She said eleven. I asked where Pioneer stood among them, and she said sixth. I told her AT&T was number one in Las Vegas out of seven carriers because my store was number one. I wasn't willing to work for a company that wasn't the best. Jodi assured me I could help bring Pioneer to the top. She reminded me I hadn't known what I was doing when I started at AT&T and that I had the opportunity to learn and grow at Pioneer just as I had at AT&T. I thought it over and eventually decided to take the leap.

I became the top banking rep in title in Las Vegas. There were nights I slept at the office at the end of the month, recording a thousand deals. It was absolute madness. The entire month would build up to the end because I worked in mortgage refinances, and people wanted to start their payments on the first of the month. Mom helped raise Sistina, providing unwavering support.

My time in title eventually led me to start Preservation West. I was approached by another mentor, the former VP of First American Title and my long-time competitor. He asked if I wanted to start a company with him, and that's how Preservation West was born. The company emerged during the 2008 market crash, focusing on maintaining foreclosures. This was my first step into the construction industry. Being a Latina woman, I never faced a language barrier since I spoke Spanish. It's a harsh truth, but speaking Spanish was a tremendous advantage in construction.

Being a Latina woman in construction was a double-edged sword. It was a blessing and a challenge. I had to earn the respect of the field workers, which made me stronger. Field operations became my forte. My unique perspective allowed me to solve problems more effectively than my male counterparts, but many men doubted my capabilities. I quickly learned that construction was all about relationships, a lesson I had learned from Mom and my previous experiences. If you do right by people, they'll do right by you. I had no prior construction experience but never faltered in my commitment to people. When I made mistakes, I always fixed them. That was a principle I learned from Mom: never screw people over, no matter what. Mom never burned bridges.

I faced adversity in my early years with Preservation West. One of the three major accounts I worked with began giving me a hard time. One day, an account manager confronted me, questioning why they should continue using me as a vendor. I responded, "You need me." He accused me of bribing people and suggested I was only getting work because I was a woman. I told him, "There's only one of me. If you want to burn the bridge, may it light your way, but it won't work out for you." They stayed with me. I was responsible for maintaining 50% of the foreclosures in town, while the other 50% was split among four vendors. I told him I deserved the work because I was the only one up at 11 pm every night, scheduling for the next morning and answering the phone at any hour. No one else had the same dedication. The next night, the account manager called, thanked me for the meeting, and said, "You're capable of more work, but for now, keep doing what you're doing." He asked if I was paying people off, but I never had to be asked for updates. I got so much work because I earned it.

As I reflect on my journey, I see a tapestry woven with threads of resilience, courage, and love. My mom's strength in fleeing Cuba, her relentless pursuit of a better life for us in America, and her unwavering support even when life was at its toughest—all these have shaped me into who I am. My dad's dreams of a brighter future, his entrepreneurial spirit, and his partnership with my mom in those early days in Chicago, also left an indelible mark on my soul.

When I reflect on the countless challenges and triumphs, I realize that every obstacle was a stepping stone. From those early days in Chicago to the bustling life in Las Vegas, from the humbling experience as a cocktail waitress to the pinnacle of my career in the construction industry, each phase taught me invaluable lessons. I learned the importance of hard work, the value of integrity, and the power of relationships.

My time with the Carranos was a crash course in humility and resilience. It taught me that no job is beneath us if it brings us closer to our goals. The relationships I built there, the respect I earned, and the fun I had, all contributed to the woman I am today. Meeting Sistina's father and becoming a mother added another layer to my identity. It strengthened my resolve to provide her with the same unwavering support and opportunities my mom gave me.

Transitioning to AT&T and meeting Jodi was a pivotal moment. It was there that I learned to navigate a new industry, to embrace change, and to believe in my ability to rise to the top. Jodi's mentorship opened doors I never knew existed and set me on a path of continued growth and success. Her faith in me reminded me of my mom's belief in my potential, reinforcing the importance of having strong, supportive figures in our lives.

Starting Preservation West during the market crash was a leap of faith. It was a testament to my ability to turn challenges into opportunities. The construction industry, with all its complexities and biases, became my arena. I had to prove myself over and over, to earn the respect of those who doubted my capabilities. But every time I stood my ground, every time I solved a problem or closed a deal, I honored the lessons I learned from my mom and dad.

As I reflect on the winding path fate has taken me down, I feel a deep sense of gratitude. Gratitude for the struggles that made me stronger, for the mentors who guided me, and for the love that fueled my journey. Sistina is now a young woman, married, full of dreams and ambitions. She carries within her the legacy of her abuelita's courage and her mother's determination. Watching her navigate her own path fills me with pride and hope.

The future is bright, not just for Sistina but for all the young Latina women who will come after us. We are breaking barriers, shattering glass ceilings, and redefining what it means to be a woman of color in America. Our stories, our struggles, and our successes are paving the way for a new generation of leaders, dreamers, and trailblazers.

The legacy of my parents' struggles and dreams lives on, not just in me and my daughter, but in every step toward freedom and justice that the Cuban people take. I am confident that the day will come when Cuba is free, and I can't wait to celebrate that victory with my family, both here and in the land that shaped us.

It was never my hair or my looks that defined me. It was the unrelenting spirit of my mom, the tenacious legacy of my dad, and the love of my daughter. It was the rich cultural heritage that flows through my veins, the resilience that runs deep in my soul, and the unwavering belief that I could create a better future. I am proud to be a Latina woman, a mother, a daughter, and a force to be reckoned with.

Valerie Carrillo

Realty One Group
Realtor

https://www.facebook.com/NormaValeriaCarrillo
https://www.instagram.com/livinglasvegasig/
https://www.zillow.com/profile/valeriasellsvegas
https://valeriecarrillo.myrealtyonegroup.com/

Living my dream as a Latina entrepreneur. I am a mother to 3 great young adults. A wife to an extremely supportive and hard working husband. My passion is empowering women by educating them on the home buying process and assuring them they can live a life without limits. Home ownership is the ultimate step in being independent and my goal is to educate women in starting their real estate portfolio. I host fun events for my clients and answer any questions they may have to move them from client to buyer. I've created "The Woman's Guide to Owning Her Dream Home," which demonstrates the step-by-step process that takes the guesswork out of how to get started. I believe a female entrepreneur is strength & bravery. You have stepped out of your comfort zone and realized your worth. You believe in yourself and ignite the fire in your soul.

Unstoppable: The Resilient Journey of a Latina Entrepreneur

By Valerie Carrillo

The journey of a Latina entrepreneur is one of resilience, courage and determination. It is a path paved with challenges, but also with immense opportunities for growth, success and legacy building. For generations, women -especially women of color- have been told to fit into predefined molds, to stay with in the boundaries of what society expects of us. But times are changing, and Latinas are stepping into our own power like never before.

To become an unstoppable Latina entrepreneur means to defy the odds, shatter stereotypes, and build something extraordinary, not just for yourself but for our community. It means embracing our culture, standing in your strength, and refusing to be limited by outdated expectations.

To my mother, my sister Melissa, my aunts and my 2 mother in laws thank you for being strong hardworking women. Thank you for being someone I can look up to and admire. I am blessed to have you all in my life. My chapter explores what it truly means to step into the power, break the glass ceiling, and claim success on your own terms.

I am a proud Latina and both of my parents are from Mexico. My father a silly but great man from Acapulco Guerrero and my mother a strong hard working woman from Chihuahua. We lived in Acapulco and right before my 3rd birthday in July of 1977 we up and moved to Las Vegas Nevada. All of us, my aunts, uncles and cousins. Everyone. They all had jobs lined up already from an uncle that was already here. I grew up in a hard working family. Right away everyone had jobs in the casinos and gourmet rooms. So much glitz and glamour. I remember being 6-7 years old and my dad would call my mother at home to tell her to bring us to the restaurant because some celebrity was there. One night at 10:30 pm she drove us down there to take picture with Dolph Lundgren that was pretty great. We had seen him in the Rocky movie. My father always had a full time job and my mother had 2 full time jobs.

Right before I started elementary school my parents saved up and bought a house. To me it was huge with a large backyard. It was the best house ever. I remember the first night we slept there all we had were blankets and a big box tv. My mother wrapped us each in a blanket and we layed in front of the tv.

One of the most powerful things a Latina entrepreneur can do is embrace our identity and use it as a source of strength. Society often portrays Latina women through limiting stereotypes either overly emotional, too strong willed, or not business minded enough. These biases can create self doubt and imposter syndrome, making it harder to feel you belong in the entrepreneurial world. But the truth is your identity is your super power. Your cultural background, bilingual abilities, work ethic, and community values set you apart in ways that are invaluable business.

I knew I wanted to be a hard worker and homeowner. I started babysitting at 11 years old. At 14 years old I started in a small greek restaurant. Later that year I worked at another fast food place. Once I turned 16 I applied at a casino restaurant and got in. A few weeks later my dad suffered a heart attack and passed away. I was now working full time and also going to school full time. It was a difficult time for me. I barely made it through school that year. Right before my senior year started my older sister and I moved out and got our own apartment. I get a lot of my strength from my mother and my older sister. We worked at the same casino, she served cocktails and I was a hostess. Now I had bills to pay. I still managed to graduate having new adult responsibilities.

Once I turned 21 years old I decided to work as a cocktail server at a downtown casino. I had a 9 month old beautiful baby girl and needed to make more money. After working there several years I realized that some of my coworkers were in their 40's, 50's and even 60's I knew I did not want to be that age and still serve cocktails. I brainstormed and decided I want to be in real estate. I took the course and then took the test. I was super excited once I got my real estate license. My first year I remember having only 1 or 2 deals all year. I was still serving cocktails full time and now had 3 babies all 4 and under and it was hard to find the time to do both. I knew I just had to give my 2 weeks notice and just do it.

In 2001 I started my real estate career. The first couple of years were good I had the support of my family and friends using my services. After they all bought it became a struggle finding new leads. I was starting to get depressed and felt defeated but I still had 3 little mouths to feed. I started going to the office everyday wether I had appointments or not. I was attending all of the meetings and any available classes. I was still struggling. I had to go back to the basics and start from the beginning. I was doing open houses again, over and over. I was working my butt off. On Sundays I would sit with my planner and figure out my week. Time blocking is something that has saved me. If I'm stuck in a rut, time block. If I'm depressed, time block. If business is slow, time block. Time blocking work, social media posting, going to the gym, journaling, praying, whatever helps you get through your day, write it down. Time blocking and going through with your plans will get you out of dark places. Time blocking will get you back on the right path.

Instead of seeing our background as an obstacle, recognize it as an asset. Not just me but many of us grew up watching our parents work tirelessly to provide for their families, sometimes juggling multiple jobs. That resilience is in our DNA.

As a Latina entrepreneur, we bring a fresh perspective to industries that desperately need diversity. The "glass ceiling" represents the invisible barriers that prevent women, especially women of color, from advancing to leadership positions or achieving their full potential. These barriers come in many forms.

When you don't see people who look like you in leadership positions, it can feel like success is out of reach. One of the most powerful ways to shatter the glass ceiling is by being visible.

I bought my first house when my kids were 3 and 1 years old. 5 years later I sold it took the equity and bought another. I wasn't the first in my family to buy a house but my mother and aunts showed me that it was possible and something I could do. I was 23 when I bought my first home and 28 when I bought my 2nd home. Now I am in my 3rd home and dream home. I was blessed to have so many amazing hard working females in my family to look up to and admire.

Every successful entrepreneur faces failures, rejections and setbacks. What sets the unstoppable ones apart is the ability to bounce back. Resilience is about seeing challenges not as roadblock but as learning experiences.

Confidence is key to breaking barriers. Many women especially us Latinas struggle with self doubt and imposter syndrome. The more you put yourself out there the more you realize you are capable.

Building a legacy is something I've longed for. Success isn't just about personal achievement, it's about paving the way for our future generations. Many of us Latina entrepreneurs start businesses not only to create our wealth but to uplift our communities, provide for our families, and inspire young girls who dream of doing the same.

Us Latinas can break cycles of financial instability and create lasting legacies.

Giving back has always been an essential part of becoming an unstoppable Latina entrepreneur. I've loved mentoring young women in the real estate industry and they have gone on to be successful women. I have provided financial opportunities for others and they have reinvested in their communities. The more we rise in business the harder it is for future generations to be ignored or underestimated.

Becoming an unstoppable Latina entrepreneur isn't about having all of the answers, it's about having the courage to take the first step and keep going.

- Own your identity and use it as your strength.
- Break the glass ceiling by demanding your place at the table.
- Cultivate an unstoppable mindset rooted in resilience and confidence.
- Build a legacy that extends beyond personal success.

The world needs more Latina entrepreneurs, leaders and change makers. Your journey isn't about you, it's about opening doors for those who will follow.

Now is the time to step into your power and make an impact. The glass ceiling is there, but you have everything it takes to shatter it.

XOXOXO TU AMIGA,
VALERIA CARRILLO

Michelle Bell

COO of She Wins Women's Network

https://www.linkedin.com/in/virtualworkwife/
https://www.facebook.com/michelle.bell.7967
https://www.instagram.com/virtualworkwife
https://virtualworkwife.com/
https://shewinswomensnetwork.com/

Hey there! I'm Michelle Bell, a professional chaos coordinator for ambitious women who refuse to choose between building an empire and being present for the moments that matter. (Spoiler alert: You can totally have both!)

As the COO of She Wins Women's Network, I help create high-impact opportunities for women to connect, collaborate, and elevate their businesses—without burning out in the process. Whether it's streamlining operations, developing growth strategies, or making sure events run like a well-oiled machine, I thrive on turning big ideas into actionable, profitable results.

Here's the thing: I don't believe in one-size-fits-all success. I'm all about tailored strategies, systems that actually work, and empowering women to step fully into their power—without the overwhelm.

At She Wins, we're building a movement where women don't just dream big—they make it happen. And I'm here to make sure they have the tools, connections, and support to do exactly that.".

The Unexpected Latina Entrepreneur

By Michelle Bell

You'd probably never guess my heritage if you ran into me on the street or at an event. A short, *very pale*, curvy redhead with a big personality, I don't exactly fit the stereotypical image of a Latina entrepreneur. No one looks at me and says, "Ah, there goes a powerhouse Latina businesswoman breaking barriers!" And yet, here I am—shattering ceilings, building businesses, and proudly carrying the strength of my Chingonas with me every step of the way.

The Invisible Latina

For most of my life, I've had to navigate what I call the "invisible Latina" experience. My fiery spirit, relentless work ethic, loud mouth, and deep love for family come from my Latina roots, but my outward appearance often confuses people.

"Hold up... you're Mexican?" is a question I've answered more times than I can count.

When I was younger, it definitely bothered me. I felt like I had to prove my heritage—justify it somehow. But as I got older, I realized that my Latina identity isn't about the way I look; it's about the way I move through the world. It's in the way I fight for my family, the way I hustle, and the way I put passion into everything I do. Being Latina isn't just about appearances or stereotypes; it's about resilience, heart, devotion, family, and an unshakable belief in building something bigger than yourself.

The Hustle Is in My DNA

Growing up, I watched my grandparents turn hard work into success, often in the face of immense challenges. My Pop taught me that nothing in life is handed to you—you have to work for it. From sunrise to sunset, he was always on his feet, making things happen. Whether it was cutting the grass, crushing cans, or cleaning the bathrooms, the man never sat down. He showed me what real work ethic is and drilled into me the value of a good day's work.

Side note: He also taught me about self-rewards. He had these end tables that were actually hidden refrigerators, and he put one on each end of the covered patio. Every Saturday, when he mowed the lawn, he would start at one end, mow a row, and sneak a beer. Then he'd mow back to the beginning and... sneak another beer. Genius!

My abuela, on the other hand, taught me what being a passenger princess was! I loved that woman, but no one—and I mean NO ONE— loved her more than Pop. He doted on her. He showed her every day in a thousand little ways that she was the most important person in the world. She never wanted for anything. And in return, she gave him four beautiful kids and a loving home.

My grandmother's name was Esperanza (Hope), and that's exactly what she was. She was sunlight in a bottle, and she made everything better. If you were sick, she would crush up your medicine in a spoonful of sugar water a la Mary Poppins. If you got a boo-boo, she would say, "It will get better before you get married," and shove you out the door with a cookie.

A few years after I got married, I was helping her make the tortillas, and one of my nieces came in crying. After a kiss and hug, Grandma said, "It will get better before you get married." I laughed and said, "Don't believe her, kid," then immediately regretted being sassy! Cue the chancla. (You flinched just now, didn't you?)

Well, she pulled an uno reverse on me. She looked me up and down, shrugged, and said, "For you, it will get better before you die." Kinda hard to refute that logic.

Hope taught me a different kind of hustle. The kind that meant your babies were clean and fed. The kind that meant loving your kids (and grandkids) was also being present in their lives, reading to them, doing homework with them, or even just having a snack while watching *Looney Toons* together. The kind that meant your a$$ was getting beat if you hid behind the brand-new curtains with three pieces of grape Bubblicious in your mouth and no control over your bubble-blowing skills!

She was the glue that held our family together, and when I close my eyes, I can still smell her perfume. The thought of her warm, soft hands makes me want to cry. I was holding her hand when she left this world, and my pop was right by her side. He went to be with her just a few weeks later. He laid down for a nap and drifted away. That same month, I lost my auntie.

Have you ever put your hand out to see what your kid will do? There are a million videos online about their reflex response. Most kids hand over their phones. Some spit out their gum. My youngest daughter has always put her hand in mine. In those moments, I am sure my abuela is touching us both. They never met, but they are forever entwined.

Hope was devoutly Catholic, and I believe this simple unconscious act by my baby girl is a promise from God that we are rooted, that our legacy of love and sacrifice lives on, and that no matter where life takes us, we will always be held by the hands that came before us.

From Military to Corporate: Pop's Legacy

My Pop had two careers. He was in the Navy, stationed at Pearl Harbor—

Oh my gosh... my mom's name is Pearl ... how did it never occur to me until today to ask about this? Note to self: Interrogate mom as soon as possible.

He gave 20 years to the Navy and retired. But not so he could enjoy life. No, he went right into a corporate gig. Honestly, I don't even think he took a vacation before starting his second career at Sony.

He was always very proud of his work ethic, and he would tell me pretty much every day that you have to get a good job with a company that offers a 401k. Working hard and saving money was the running theme of my childhood.

"Put 10% in savings, 10% in your 401k, and plan for your future." Oh, how I wish I had paid more attention to his advice! But I got caught up in simply surviving the corporate world. No shade on Pop, but he kinda failed to tell me how sucky corporate life would be.

And so, after five years of working for the man, I blew that popsicle stand and started my own business. I had no clients, no investors, and sooo much fear of failing. But I also had a ton of grit. I knew how to pivot when things got tough. I knew how to work harder than anyone else in the room. And I knew that if I failed, I'd get back up again—because that's what my family had always done.

But I'm jumping ahead a little bit. We should probably talk about ...

My Summers as a "Migrant" Worker

Slightly political rant in 3, 2, 1...

If you've spent your whole life walking on paved sidewalks and streets, then you have no business talking about "who will do the jobs no one else wants." You don't have the real-world experience to understand what it means to endure a growing season—to watch the land dictate your livelihood, to feel the weight of uncertainty with every harvest—and maybe even to build a future from the literal ground up.

So, next time you hear "who will do the jobs no one else wants"—Hi, it's me. This girl. Right here. Me and every other teenager being raised in a farming community.

Every summer, I hauled my lily-white behind out to the fields to pick strawberries, spinach, cucumbers, or whatever was in rotation that year. This was back before sunscreen was a girl's best friend, and the minimum wage was $3.35 per hour. Yes, you read that right. $3.35 per hour, and we didn't get paid until the end of the season!

Let me save you the mental gymnastics of doing that math. It was 1981. While other kids were hanging out at the mall or obsessing over the launch of MTV, I was lucky enough to be working the fields six days a week, rain or shine.

If you're having flashbacks of that movie *Children of the Corn*... I feel you, bestie! Teenage boys can make anything into a nightmare, especially if you're a four-foot-tall girl in a field of six-foot chard! But I wouldn't trade those summers or the experience for anything in the world. It's the truest form of hustle culture I've ever known.

While I was busting my a$$ in the fields, my mom was turning her hobbies into what would eventually become a high six-figure quilting business. My grandmother had taught all of us how to sew, knit, and crochet over the years. I got my first sewing machine when I was five. That and a bag of scrap materials and some baby doll patterns. There's no need to buy things if you can make them yourself. Everything can be upcycled into something new.

And for people who don't sew or knit, there's a certain novelty in buying things that are handmade. My mom saw that and took advantage of it. She paid attention to the people around her, what they liked, what their hobbies were, and then she would create these incredible sweaters or blankets that depicted scenes of hunting, bowling, or other such things.

She started quilting, and things just took off from there. She eventually patented her own line of tools and published multiple patterns. She even began traveling to teach her methods all over the world. Not bad for a teen mom who survived some of the most terrifying DV stories you can imagine.

But that's her story to tell, though I doubt she ever will. Sometimes grit means putting it behind you and never ever opening that door again.

Navigating the Boys' Club

The experience and work ethic I gained working those summers have stuck with me throughout my career. I learned early on that the corporate world is just as much a boys' club as farming or high school, but when you add being a woman—especially a Latina woman—to the mix, the obstacles multiply. I've sat in rooms where I was the only woman. I've been talked over, underestimated, and dismissed. I've had my ideas repeated back to me by men as if they'd come up with them first (oh, the joys of having my own proposals "mansplained" to me).

And when I left corporate America to escape the boys' club, I landed right in the middle of something just as bad—the "bro marketing" world. In the early days of internet marketing, the loudest voices, the so-called "gurus," were all men pushing the same recycled theories about "what sells." Sure, people were making money, but the tactics felt slimy, manipulative, and exhausting. It was all high-pressure, fear-based scarcity tactics—less about connection and more about squeezing every last dollar out of people.

Then, slowly, the women started emerging. The "lifestyle" marketers, the ones who made six-figure businesses look effortless, all while posing with their Dolce's and purse puppies. But let's be real—it was still just bro marketing wrapped in a prettier, perfume-drenched package. The same pressure, the same scarcity, but with better lighting and a curated aesthetic.

That's not me. It's not my vibe. I don't do cookie-cutter strategies, and I don't believe in selling dreams with no substance. I built my business on authenticity, connection, and actually giving a damn about the people I serve. Because real success—the kind that lasts—comes from building relationships, not just revenue streams. It comes from having a heart of service and embracing what makes us unique. I was never just building a business for myself—I was carving a path for other women, other Latinas, and the daughters and granddaughters who come after me.

Redefining Latina Success

One of the biggest misconceptions I've had to challenge is the narrow definition of what a Latina entrepreneur *should* look like. Too often, the media presents a singular image of success—one that doesn't include women like me. But success doesn't come in just one shade, one accent, one background. Success looks like women showing up authentically, taking risks, and owning their space in the world.

And let's talk about the stereotypes for a second—because I refuse to buy into them, and I sure as hell won't live *down* to them. I don't have to be spicy or fiery to be taken seriously. I don't need to be bootylicious, and I don't have to prove my worth by grinding myself into the ground. I don't have to package myself into what people expect a Latina entrepreneur to be—loud but likable, bold but not *too* bold, successful but still playing small. No, gracias.

For me, success isn't about revenue or social media metrics. It's about impact. It's about creating opportunities not just for myself but for others. It's about proving that women entrepreneurs don't have to fit into a box—screw the box! Blow up the damn box already. We can be bold, unconventional, and *unexpected*. Because the real power of being a woman—a Latina woman—isn't in meeting someone else's expectations; it's in rewriting the rules altogether.

Lessons from a Latina Entrepreneur

1. **Own Your Identity** – You don't have to fit someone else's mold. Your background, your experiences, your culture—these are your strengths. Embrace them.

2. **Hustle Smart, Not Just Hard** – Hard work is a given, but smart work is the game-changer. Learn to delegate, automate, and prioritize what actually moves the needle.

3. **Build Your Own Table** – If the doors aren't opening for you, build your own damn door. If the seats at the table are taken, create your own space and invite other women into it!

4. **Find Your People** – Community is everything. Surround yourself with mentors, allies, and people who will lift you up. And be the kind of woman who lifts up the next one. You are not an island, and success is rarely achieved in a silo.

5. **Be Relentless** – Obstacles will come. People will doubt you. You might even doubt yourself. It's ok to throw yourself a momentary pity party and move on. Nobody cares. Work harder.

A Legacy of Strength

When I look back at my journey, I see more than just the businesses I've built or the books I've written. I see generations of resilient women who worked tirelessly to create better lives for their families. I see my abuela's hands, soft and caring, and I think about how she would smile knowing that her granddaughter is making waves in a world that wasn't always built for her.

I may not look like the "typical" Latina entrepreneur. But my heart, my fire, my drive? They are 1000% Latina. And with that, I'll keep breaking glass ceilings, not just for myself but for every woman who dares to dream big.

The Path Forward

My journey has taught me that authenticity is our superpower. When we lean into our unique experiences and perspectives, we bring something to the table that nobody else can. That's not just good for business—it's revolutionary.

Some might think being a homemaker wasn't the most ambitious or inspiring thing my grandma Hope could have done. But she wasn't just a mother, a sister, or an abuela—she *was* hope itself. The living, breathing proof that love, grit, and unwavering determination could build something greater than the circumstances we were born into.

The women of my family are made of her sacrifice, her strength, and her unshakable belief in something better. We don't just carry hope—we *are* Hope.

So to all the unexpected Latina entrepreneurs out there—the ones who don't fit the stereotype, the ones who are blazing their own trails—I see you. Keep pushing boundaries. Keep redefining what it means to be a Latina in business. Your voice matters. Your story matters.

My hope for you is that you never shrink yourself to fit someone else's definition of success. That you own your story, your roots, and your power unapologetically. That you chase your dreams with the same fire that burned in the women who came before you. And that when you break through your own glass ceilings, you reach back and pull another woman up with you. Because we are not just walking through doors— we are building new ones. And that is the legacy of Hope.

Sonia Rodrigues

Transition to Wellness
Psychotherapist & Life Transition Coach

https://www.linkedin.com/in/sonia-rodrigues-48b87149/
https://www.facebook.com/SoniaRodriguesLPC/
https://instagram.com/transition.to.wellness
http://www.transitiontowellness.com/
https://soniarodrigues-marto.tribesites.com/

Sonia Rodrigues has been a licensed psychotherapist for over 20 years. She is the owner of a psychotherapy and coaching practice called Transition to Wellness. She has worked with people of all ages, helping them navigate various challenges in their life. She utilizes a holistic approach and provides a safe and supportive environment where her clients can feel supported on their path towards healing from their traumatic experiences and guided towards creating the life they desire. She provides individual therapy, coaching and also offers a variety of workshops on topics related to trauma, post-traumatic growth and fostering resilience.

Rising Above: Overcoming Challenges in the Entrepreneurial World

By Sonia Rodrigues

Opening Reflections: The Foundations of Dreaming Big

From a young age, I lived in an environment where resources were scarce, and every opportunity felt like a distant dream. I will never forget the moment when I was five years old and my parents bought a foreclosed house. The windows were boarded up, and the inside was a chaotic mess with rubble scattered across the rooms. I stood there, wide-eyed, and thought to myself, "This is our home?" My parents, though overwhelmed by the massive task ahead of them, were ecstatic. To them, it was a dream come true—finally owning a home in the U.S. after years of hard work and sacrifice. But for me, while I respected their perseverance, I couldn't shake the feeling that I wanted more from life. I longed to break free from the cycle of financial struggles, to experience a life filled with opportunity and freedom.

Desire for More: The Seed of Ambition

Growing up, I was incredibly fortunate to have hardworking parents who managed what little we had with diligence and care. Their ability to save for a rainy day gave us a sense of security, but deep down, I knew that I wanted more than just survival—I wanted to thrive. I wanted a life where I didn't have to constantly worry about money. I yearned for experiences beyond the limitations of my upbringing: traveling, dining at different restaurants, or simply having the freedom to explore the world without fear of financial constraints. I immersed myself in books, seeking knowledge, constantly asking myself, *How do others achieve these experiences without living in financial stress?*

This hunger for more was not just about luxury—it was about accessing possibilities, finding the doors that others had walked through to create lives of abundance and joy.

Balancing Family and Ambition

My parents, as immigrants, had dreams for me that were rooted in hard work and stability. They envisioned a future where I could secure a job that promised benefits, stability, and financial security. Their dream for me was grounded in the values of resilience and duty, which they had carried from their own struggles.

However, my dreams didn't always align with theirs. In high school, I threw myself into everything—from sports to drama to running for student council—and worked two part-time jobs. My parents, though proud of my hard work, worried that I wasn't dedicating enough time to family. I struggled to balance these desires: to experience the world beyond my immediate environment while honoring the importance of family connections. This conflict would later extend into my college years, where I wanted the full, independent college experience, while they expected me to stay close to home. I knew I wanted to experience more and to be surrounded with others who wanted to do big things. That's where it all started and before you knew it, I was traveling to Europe to study abroad and continued to create experiences where I could keep learning and growing and embracing a life filled with opportunities.

Pursuing Education and Building Resilience

When I first went off to college, I was the first in my extended family to leave home for higher education. My parents' sacrifices meant that I had the opportunity to follow my passion and further my education. College became a space of growth, where I threw myself into every opportunity—from clubs to volunteer work, and even working part-time to help fund my studies. Balancing all of this while still keeping close ties to my family was an ongoing challenge, but it shaped the foundation of the balance I still strive to achieve today: a balance between ambition, family, and relationships. This continues to be at the forefront of my life, and it is a constant challenge. Finding time for it all is not easy but being mindful of all of the different ways in which it can be achieved is crucial for your growth and your well-being.

The Pull of Entrepreneurship

As I worked my way through college and into my career, I realized that my desires were shifting toward something greater: the freedom to create, to build, and to lead. I found myself drawn to entrepreneurship, an area my immigrant parents had never fully embraced. In their view, entrepreneurship was a risky endeavor, one that threatened the stability they had worked so hard to achieve. But for me, entrepreneurship represented freedom—the ability to shape my future, take risks, and create opportunities for myself and others.

I pursued my degree in counseling and worked my way up in a large state university, where I found opportunities to grow and innovate. I created new mental health programs, eventually managing a team that grew from 12 to over 200 employees. But despite this success, I always found myself asking, *What's next?* The entrepreneurial spirit within me continued to pull me forward, and I knew I had to take that leap, so I started my own private therapy practice. However, as I worked with clients in therapy, I realized that many of the challenges they faced were not just about mental health, but also about life transitions and personal growth. This sparked a desire in me to expand my services beyond traditional therapy. I began offering life transition coaching, helping individuals navigate major life changes such as career shifts, relationship changes, and personal development. I also started creating workshops designed to empower others with the tools and skills they needed to overcome obstacles and thrive in their personal and professional lives.

As my practice grew, I felt compelled to share my knowledge and experiences on a larger scale. I began writing books and articles focused on resilience, personal growth, and overcoming adversity, with the goal of reaching people who might not have access to traditional therapy. Writing allowed me to extend my impact beyond one-on-one sessions, offering guidance and inspiration to a broader audience. My mission evolved to include not just providing therapy but offering resources for women looking to build resilience, pursue their dreams, and navigate the challenges of life with confidence.

Building on this vision, I started working on a women's membership program, a community designed to support and encourage women on their entrepreneurial journeys and personal growth. This program is centered around creating a network of like-minded women who can share experiences, provide mentorship, and empower one another to succeed.

This year, I've set my sights on expanding my reach even further. Public speaking has become a key focus of my business goals, as I want to inspire and encourage women through conferences, workshops, and speaking engagements. One of my ultimate aspirations is to deliver a TEDx talk, where I can share my message of resilience, overcoming obstacles, and empowering others to take action towards their dreams. I know that the power of connection and community is the key to fostering growth, and I want to continue to amplify that message. With each new step, my goal remains clear: to support and encourage other women to tap into their potential, to rise above their challenges, and to achieve the dreams they've always had. By expanding my platform and reaching more women, I hope to create lasting impact and help foster a culture of resilience, courage, and empowerment.

To every woman reading this, I want to remind you that the power to create the life and business you desire is within you. The first step in this journey is to create a clear vision of where you want to go. Your vision is your compass—it keeps you focused, especially when the road gets tough. Take the time to reflect on what truly excites you, what aligns with your values, and what your life's purpose is. From there, break that vision down into manageable, achievable goals. It's easy to feel overwhelmed by the magnitude of your dreams, but remember that success is built one step at a time. Start by setting small, actionable goals that move you closer to the larger picture. Celebrate the wins along the way, no matter how small, because they are all steps toward something bigger. Surround yourself with people who support your vision, who cheer you on when you feel like giving up, and who hold you accountable to your dreams. Pursue each goal with persistence and patience. Trust that with every effort you make, you are building the foundation of something incredible. You have the strength, resilience, and ability to not only dream but to make those dreams a reality. Take it one step at a time, and you will get there.

Navigating Financial Barriers and Resource Limitations

Starting a business with little to no money was challenging to say the least. I carried the weight of my family's financial struggles with me as I launched my practice. Without significant savings, connections, or a strong network, I was forced to think creatively. I sought out free business workshops, consumed podcasts, and networked relentlessly, connecting with anyone who might offer advice. Listening to anything related to starting and growing a business was something I always had in the background. I knew this was something I knew little about, so I had to start with information gathering.

Despite my dedication, progress was slow. I began working long hours, sacrificing my health and family time in an attempt to grow my business. Soon, I realized that burnout was inevitable unless I learned to prioritize self-care and sustainable growth. I didn't have to do it all alone. One of the most important lessons I learned along the way was the value of seeking out affordable resources to help grow my business without overextending myself financially. As a small business owner with limited capital, I couldn't afford expensive consultants or large-scale marketing campaigns, but that didn't mean I was without options. I started by taking advantage of free workshops, webinars, and online courses that were readily available. There are countless resources out there—many of them completely free or low-cost—that can help you build your knowledge, streamline your processes, and improve your skillset. I found networking groups, like She Rises Studios, where women entrepreneurs shared not only their experiences but also valuable resources, tips, and tools for managing business operations on a budget. I also sought out mentorship from experienced entrepreneurs who were willing to share their insights and guide me without charging hefty fees. Additionally, many government programs, non-profits, and local organizations offer grants, low-interest loans, and affordable services specifically designed for small businesses. I learned to leverage these resources, finding ways to support my business growth without sacrificing my health, my time, or my peace of mind. It became clear that in the world of entrepreneurship, asking for help and seeking out the right resources is just as important as hard work. By using the available tools at my disposal, I was able to grow my business in a way that was both sustainable and manageable without burning myself out.

The Power of Connection: Building a Support System

It wasn't until I joined the She Rises Studios networking group that I truly understood the value of surrounding myself with like-minded, driven women. I had spent so much time trying to be everything for everyone—taking on every task, managing all the details—that I had forgotten one fundamental truth: growth happens in community. The journey of entrepreneurship can feel incredibly isolating at times, but when you connect with others who are walking similar paths, you realize you're not alone. By surrounding myself with women who were navigating the same challenges, I found not only the support but also the motivation I needed to continue pushing forward. These women became my mentors, allies, and sounding boards, offering wisdom, advice, and encouragement that I hadn't even known I needed. What I learned is that mentorship doesn't always come from a single individual—it can come from an entire network of women who share their experiences and guidance, allowing you to learn from each other's successes and failures.

Having a strong support system has been instrumental in my growth. These women helped me see my blind spots, pushed me outside of my comfort zone, and reminded me of my value when self-doubt crept in. They were there to celebrate my wins, no matter how small, and to help me regroup when I encountered setbacks. More than just offering advice, they offered camaraderie, a safe space to be vulnerable and share my struggles without fear of judgment. This connection fostered a sense of belonging that made the entrepreneurial journey feel less daunting and more like a collective mission. Through this community, I began to understand the true power of collaboration. Success does not have to be a solitary pursuit; it can be a shared experience that thrives when you have a network of women who genuinely care about your growth and want to see you succeed. When you invest in building meaningful relationships with mentors and peers, you unlock a wealth of knowledge and strength that accelerates your personal and professional development. Together, we can achieve so much more than we ever could alone.

Turning Cultural Heritage Into an Advantage

One of the most profound lessons I've learned is the importance of embracing my heritage. As the daughter of immigrant parents, I grew up with strong values of hard work, respect, and community. At times, I felt pressured to conform to a mold that didn't fully resonate with me. But as I ventured further into entrepreneurship, I came to realize that my cultural identity was an asset and a true testament to my growth and success. My trilingualism, my understanding of diverse communities, and my connection to my roots all gave me a unique perspective that allowed me to create a business that truly reflected who I was while also allowing me to connect with a diverse group of women, many of whom shared similar goals and dreams.

Overcoming Self-Doubt and Staying True to My Vision

The path to success was never linear, and I constantly wrestled with self-doubt. At times, I wondered if someone like me—someone from a working-class, immigrant background—could truly succeed in an entrepreneurial world dominated by those with more resources. But with each step, I reminded myself of why I was doing this—not just for me, but for others who might see themselves in my story.

The first and most crucial step in achieving your goals is to have a clear and well-defined vision. This vision serves as your roadmap, guiding you through every challenge and decision along the way. It's essential that your vision is detailed and clear, but also aligned with who you truly are and what you believe your life's purpose to be. When your goals reflect your values, passions, and deeper purpose, they become more than just aspirations—they become a calling. Taking the time to map out this vision, ensuring that it resonates with your authentic self, will give you the focus and drive needed to overcome obstacles and stay on course. Your vision is the foundation upon which you will build your success, and when it is in harmony with your purpose, it will propel you toward the future you have always dreamed of, with clarity, confidence, and unwavering commitment.

Empowering Others: Giving Back to the Community

Now, as I reflect on my journey, I'm filled with pride not only for the success I've achieved but for the opportunity to help others achieve theirs. I mentor interns and women entrepreneurs, sharing my story and offering the guidance I wish I had received early on. By lifting others, we can create a community of women who are not just participants in the entrepreneurial world, but leaders and changemakers.

Here are some tips I've learned along my journey that can help you take the first steps or move forward toward achieving your goals:

- **Believe in Your Potential:** One of the most powerful lessons I've learned is the importance of believing in yourself. Confidence in your abilities can carry you through even the toughest challenges. There will be times when the world tells you "no" or when doubt creeps in, but trust me, if you stay connected to your vision and believe that you are capable, you will rise above any obstacle. Keep pushing forward, even when it feels impossible.

- **Surround Yourself with the Right People:** Building a strong support network has been essential to my success. I can't emphasize enough how important it is to connect with others—especially women who share big dreams like you do. Seek out mentors, peers, and allies who have walked a similar path. The right people can offer guidance, support, and inspiration, helping you learn faster and navigate the ups and downs of entrepreneurship with more confidence.

- **Create a Clear and Detailed Plan of Action:** One of the things that kept me moving forward was having a detailed plan. Breaking down my bigger goals into smaller, intentional steps kept me on track. Whether it was learning a new skill, investing in my business, or seeking guidance, I learned that consistent progress—no matter how small—leads to lasting success. It's about staying focused and being deliberate with your actions. Don't worry about being perfect, just keep moving forward.

- **Build a Community of Women in Business:** Entrepreneurship doesn't have to be a lonely road. Surrounding myself with like-minded, ambitious women has been one of the most rewarding parts of my journey. When you connect with others who understand your struggles and share your goals, you create a space for collaboration, encouragement, and growth. This community has helped me stay motivated, inspired, and accountable—and it can do the same for you. Together, we can accomplish so much more than we can alone.

Conclusion: The Journey Continues

As I reflect on my journey, I recognize that it has been filled with both challenges and triumphs. There have been setbacks—times when it felt like the weight of the world was pressing down—but there has also been incredible growth, both personally and professionally. The beauty of this journey lies not in avoiding obstacles but in learning to navigate through them with resilience and unwavering determination. Every hurdle I've faced has brought me one step closer to the person I am becoming. And while I know new challenges will continue to arise, I've learned that with the right support system and a community of women who are committed to breaking barriers and lifting each other up, success becomes an inevitable outcome. I have seen how quickly I have grown the minute I got in the room with the right group of women.

The power of sisterhood cannot be overstated. As women, we are an unstoppable force when we unite, supporting and encouraging one another to reach our full potential. We rise together, not by competing against each other, but by recognizing that there is enough space for all of us to thrive. This journey is not meant to be walked alone. It's about finding strength in community, learning from one another, and celebrating each other's victories. When we stand together, we are empowered to shatter the limitations placed on us and create the lives and businesses we've always dreamed of.

I want you to understand that the key to success isn't just about financial achievements or recognition. It's about developing confidence in your ability to reach your goals, no matter how daunting they may seem. It's about knowing that the true measure of success is in the courage to overcome personal and professional obstacles and in staying true to your vision, even when the path ahead is unclear. Your dreams are valid, and with determination, passion, and the support of others, you have the power to turn them into reality.

Above all, I hope that reading this has shown you the importance of building connections with other women who will cheer you on, offer their wisdom, and walk beside you as you grow. No matter your background, your story, or where you start, know that you are capable of achieving everything you set your heart on. And as you rise, remember that you are not only paving the way for your own success but for the next generation of women who will follow in your footsteps. Together, we are unstoppable. Keep dreaming, keep growing, and always remember—you are never alone in this journey. The women who have gone before you and the ones who walk alongside you are all rooting for your success.

Anna Barboza Lugo

Pure Tea Love & Pure CBD Love
Owner, Author, Mentor, Facilitator

https://www.linkedin.com/in/anna-lugo-62746219/
https://www.facebook.com/profile.php?id=61550876111683
https://www.instagram.com/Alohalugo/
https://www.puretealove.com/

My name is Anna Lugo and I Am a Child of God, A Prayer Warrior, A Single Mother, a Sister, a Friend, An Encourager, A Mentor, a Retired I.T. Professional, and a Daughter of the King. I am also a business Owner of Pure Teal Love and Pure CBD Luv. I'm a Tea'V Host on EveryDay Woman TV Network where I have a show called "We Have A Tea For That... Positivi-Tea".

I also manage a Facebook page called "Up2UGod". I organically created this page 10 years ago where I'm dedicated to sharing a word of encouragement on a daily basis. This page recently reached 2.7 millions Souls over a 28 day cycle, I am so blessed that God is using me in this Way. I am also a license plate whisper and have seen hundreds of Spiritual Plates. I post these plates with music on my newly created tiktok page.

My Motto in Life is, "I'm Too Blessed To Be Stressed" and If Its To Be' Its Up To Me'. My goal is to Encourage / Inspire one at least one person a Day!

My Ten-Cent Raise!

By Anna Barboza Lugo

I'm a retired Latina professional with a rich background of 40 years in technology, implementing complex data networks and telecommunications. I have consistently experienced growth in my career by focusing on my Leadership skills and leveraging my experience with mentorship programs and entrepreneurship opportunities. In the last five years since retirement in 2020, I've been blessed to start two businesses and become a Best Selling Author.

Thinking back to the early 80s, when I first moved to San Jose, I purchased my first Leadership book at a garage sale for a quarter. The book was called *See You At The Top*. This book left an impression on me and my growth as a newly hungry leader. I learned that there is no elevator to the top. You must take the stairs one at a time. These steps required me to keep my "stinking thinking" at bay and taking each step would demand a determined action, consistency, perseverance, persistence, discipline, determination and hard work.

This was at the beginning of my journey and newly found passion when I discovered I wanted to learn the traits and characteristics of a successful woman in business. I was self-taught and made it a daily habit to introduce and pour Positivi-Tea into my daily practice by reading books and listening to audio books on my drive to work. I read Og Mandino books, went to Zig Zigler conferences and attended some Anthony/Tony Robbins seminars. Also read *How to Think and Grow Rich*. I had a passion for learning Leadership skills and was positively impacted by some of the greatest motivational speakers at that time.

I recall a time when working at Longs Drug store, and I had noticed I had received a raise. It was all of ten cents. So, I thought, *WOW, I need to speak to my manager to ask why such a little raise*. I went to his office, and he was on the phone. Once he was off the phone, he invited me into his office and asked me what I wanted. I proceeded to tell him, I noticed I had a 10 cent raise and his response was... So, what about it? I said it was only ten cents... And his response was "I didn't need to give you anything." I was taken aback by his cold-hearted demeanor and disrespectful mannerisms, so I said I felt I was worth more because he gave me more responsibilities. Like ordering candy and cosmetics, and always putting me on the busiest station. I told him I'm a single mother trying to make a living and my entire $69.00 a week checks were going to the babysitter. He said, "Are we done here? I have things to do. Like I said, I didn't have to give you anything."

I left his office and went straight to the shipping department and told my girlfriend/co-worker that we are having happy hour. That I just had it with the poor management and needed to vent.

We ended up at a Mexican restaurant and that's where I was telling my girlfriend what had happened with the boss. I was clearly unhappy with the ten-cent raise, but especially for the disrespect shown and my hard work being unnoticed. It fueled me to no end.

What I did not realize is that this man and his wife sitting next to me overheard my story about my ten-cent raise.

At that time my girlfriend went to the ladies' room, and this nice gentleman proceeded to introduce himself. He turned out to be a gentleman by the name of Richard Cornejo, who was the Human Resource Director for a company called Racal Vadic. He said their company was growing and they had several open positions, and he asked me to call him on Monday. He was going to set an interview with the Hiring Manager. They needed a receptionist and said I would be a great representation of the company's front desk. He said greeting visitors and making calls would be fairly easy work and requires someone who has personality and tenacity.

I just couldn't believe that God put this person in my path, and certainly couldn't wait for Monday to start the process of meeting with the Hiring Manager.

I went to the interview and was told I was the top runner for the position. However, they still had two more interviews and a decision would be made fairly soon. So, I thought to myself, that I would give a 2 weeks' notice at Longs and wait for the call from Racal Vadic. Lesson #1: Never quit a job until you have an offer letter. Well, it turned out that I did not get the receptionist job. When they called to tell me I was shocked and had already given my 2 weeks' notice. So needless to say, I had to ask for my job back. The manager told me he did not have any openings and I would be on call if anyone calls in sick, then I would be the backup person. So, I looked for other stores to be transferred to. In the meantime, Racal Vadic calls me back and says they want to interview me for another position as a Mail Clerk for their new office building in Milpitas. I went on the interview and was once again told I was the front runner for the job, but I didn't want to get my high hopes up in case they were interested in conducting more interviews. When I received the call that I did get the job, I was so excited. It was the breakthrough I finally needed. I have Mr. Cornejo to thank for that.

It was an exciting time, my first corporate job. I learned so much at this company and I was getting 25 cent raises on nearly every paycheck for the first 6 months. I ran the new mail room for about a year, when my boss, Faye Rysland, asked me if I wanted to learn how to install phones. My immediate response was YES!! She then said our PBX technician gave a month's notice. I was to stick by his side to learn everything I could for the next month. He would go on to teach me and first showed me how to get an extension number, program a single line phone, (two wire line) and a multi-line (four wire), phone lines, punch down the wires. When I did it for the first time, I immediately felt a sense of accomplishment. To hear dial tone, once I plugged the phone into the wall, was the greatest feeling ever. My goal from then on was to be a sponge and learn every aspect of the telecom world. It was so intriguing to me and my new found passion was born. It was like a big jigsaw puzzle putting the pieces together in learning how to build a switch from the ground up. I started attending the Introduction to Telecommunications courses. Intro to voice and data networks and infrastructure. I started learning about FCC standards and integrations.

I later left Racal Vadic and went to work at Northern Telecom, the manufacturer of the telephone switch I had been learning. When I was hired by Northern Telecom, I was to support 79 accounts in the San Jose Bay area. However, before they would put me in the field, I had to be certified on their PBX switches. They sent me to Plano, Texas, for six weeks of training. I had my daughter at the time, who was three years old. Fortunately, my mother lived in Texas at the time so I was able to take my daughter on our journey of starting a new career. To finally land a job in Telecommunications with a real salary. I had come a long way since my $69.00 checks at Longs to finally having my first salaried position.

I stayed at Northern Telecom for a few years until a new opportunity popped up and Northrop relocated me and my daughter to Southern California. We stayed in California for a year and then moved back to Silicon Valley. When I returned to San Jose, I found a position as a Technical Support Engineer at a voice messaging company called VMX. It was here at VMX where I accepted a position with a private company and negotiated a much higher salary. It was the first time I was awarded company stock as an incentive. I then worked for a company called Octel, which later merged with Lucent Technologies and later spun off as a separate company called Avaya. We were forced to cash out our stock and the money was spent on purchasing my home 27 years ago in Las Vegas.

After 17 years of working my way up in my career, I was let go due to a workforce reduction at the company. While at Avaya I held many positions, starting as a Sales Engineer, a Product Engineer, and even traveled internationally to collect specifications to support power and tone cadence for the integrations of the telephone voice messaging equipment. I loved being an International Product Manager. It allowed me to expand my knowledge about other countries and cultures. Once I was given my pink slip, things changed and life took a different turn. I found myself immersed in many trials, tribulations and challenges. I went through a divorce, moved back to Los Angeles for a year, then finally moved to Las Vegas, where I had rental property that was empty. So, I decided it was time to move out of LA and make Las Vegas my home.

Since moving to Las Vegas 21 years ago, I got my first job as Telecommunications Project Manager at Harrah's Entertainment, and then went to MGM as a contractor, then worked at IGT, then went back to MGM as a permanent employee and worked on City Center. I went through a one-year mentorship program while at MGM and earned a Distinguished Leadership Award. Every year, I attended the Women's Leadership Conference. I stayed working at MGM Resorts International until Friday, March 13, 2020. That was when COVID shut the world down.

Later that year on my daddy's birthday on 11/11/2020, we (my daughter and I), launched my first company called Pure CBD Love. I started taking CBD in 2018 when my daughter was in a horrific car accident and I needed to combat my stress, anxiety, inflammation and insomnia. I found this to be my daily medicine. Our company slogan is "We Are Healers Not Dealers" and we believe "CBD Is Hope Not Dope."

I now had a newfound passion, learning about CBD, the benefits behind the products, and the wellness aspects of taking these products. I just love teaching others about the misconceptions of hemp, THC, and CBD.

I self-taught myself and attended 100 episodes of the ABC's to CBD. I learned so much about this God-given plant and the many benefits. This put me in the cannabis industry, and my mission is to help educate clients who suffer from chronic pain, severe stress, inflammation and insomnia.

Then in 2023, my pages disappeared on social media and my website was gone. So, I decided to focus my attention on the educational side and start offering courses to be certified in CBD and Wellness.

On 2/22/22, I launched Pure Tea Love, our sister company, and created our slogan: "We Have A Tea For That... Positivi-Tea!"

I wrote my first chapter in an anthology, *Everyday Woman's Guide to Living Your Best Life*. My chapter is called "Spirituali-Tea Is My Priori-Tea for Eterni-Tea!"

In 2024, I launched my "Tea'V Show," called *We Have A Tea For That... Positivi-Tea!* I also started a social media page called "Women Inspiring Women" and will be offering certified spirituality coaching courses. It will also be a place for new membership opportunities with She Wins Women's Network.

I will be releasing my first solo book on 11/11/25 called, *We Have A Tea For That...*

In February 2025, I released my second anthology called *Pray, Don't Panic: A Path to Inner Calm*. My chapter is called "Everything is Up2UGod!" Because I believe everything is up to Him.

When I first moved to Las Vegas 21 years ago, my first personalized license plate was Up2UGod. I even had a Facebook page that reached 2.7 million souls in August of 2023.

I am also very thrilled and excited to create a space for Latinas, Senoritas and my Bonita Amigas. I plan to call it "Latina's Inspiring La'Tea'Nas!!"

My goal since becoming a single mother in 1979 has always been to become a financially independent woman and mother, and to raise a positive child in a negative world. I can say I have successfully achieved that goal. I worked hard all my adult life and had several important facets to making a positive difference, a positive impact and was blessed to have had many mentors and role models along the way cheering me on by my side. The journey continues as I ride the ships in life: Mentorship, Leadership, Friendship, Relationship, Entrepreneurship, Worship, Fellowship, Companionship and Partnership.

I am also thankful for a leadership course I took 16 years ago, where I discovered my limited beliefs and had to break through many barriers that were standing in my way of accomplishing my goals, my dreams and my desire to achieve wealth, health and strong leadership and mentoring coaching.

I went through 100 days of leadership where I would Dream, Declare, and Deliver, three tasks every day by 9:00 a.m., then clear the tasks off my plate by 9:00 p.m. When you hold yourself accountable and show up for yourself, you see it in this one particular task. It's an integrity test with yourself. How often do you keep your word with yourself? How are you showing up for YOU?

Gone are the days of ten-cent raises and where trying to survive on $69.00 was a norm.

Life is going to do what life does. It's going to rise. It's going to fall. It's going to be beautiful. It's going to be tragic. It's going to be mundane. It's going to be chaotic. Time is going to do what time does. It's going to move slowly. It's going to move at lightning speed. There will be moments where you feel like you have too much time on your hands and there will be other moments when you don't have nearly enough time or money.

People are going to do what people do. They're going to breathe life into you. They're going to knock the wind out of you. They're going to disappoint. They're going to excite. They're going to surprise you—and inspire in the best and worst ways.

But God is also going to do what God does. He's going to guide. He's going to comfort. He's going to direct. He's going to lead. He's going to sustain. He's going to provide. He's going to forgive. He's going to heal. And he's going to love us and ordain our every step. I truly believe He does not call the qualified, He qualifies the Called. He certainly called and qualified this Latina, and for that I'm thankful, grateful and blessed.

Dr. Manuela Jimenez, Ed.D

Educational Leader

https://www.linkedin.com/in/drmanuela/
https://www.facebook.com/Dr.Manuela.Jimenez
https://www.instagram.com/dr.manuela.jimenez/
https://www.magcloud.com/browse/issue/3002391
https://hollywoodbusiness.com/2025/02/06/doctor-nela-shattering-glass-ceilings-from-the-classroom-to-the-runway/

Dr. Manuela Jimenez, Ed.D, is an inspiring educational leader dedicated to transforming learning for all. As a certified school principal, teacher, author, and mentor, she passionately advocates for equitable education. In 2025, she was crowned Dr. World Latina, using her platform to promote gender equality in leadership, emphasized by her runway debut at New York Fashion Week alongside Miss Universe 2024.

Her contributions to educational leadership and fashion earned her a spot in the 2025 edition of Marquis Who's Who in America. In 2024, she was honored with the Young Athena Professional Award for her efforts in empowering women's leadership. Additionally, she serves as a peer reviewer for the Taylor & Francis Journal of Educational Leadership and shares her insights at national conferences, inspiring educators and students alike.

Outside of her professional commitments, she enjoys traveling with her family, embodying her belief that learning and adventure have no limitations.

The Triumphs and Trials of a Latina Entrepreneur in Education Leadership

By Dr. Manuela Jimenez, Ed.D

Women rule the world. It's not really worth fighting because they know what they're doing. Ask Napoleon. Ask Adam. Ask Richard Burton or Richie Sambora. Many a man has crumbled.
—Jon Bon Jovi

As a Latina entrepreneur, I embarked on a journey that brought me to a crossroads where my dreams collided with various challenges. I navigated a landscape often filled with societal biases that sometimes felt overwhelming. Each step forward was accompanied by both anticipation and adversity, shaping my path in unexpected ways. Nevertheless, I persevered through every challenge I faced, driven by my intrinsic passion for everything I do.

Throughout my fifteen years in education, I have dedicated myself wholeheartedly as a teacher, investing my energy in nurturing young minds and fostering an inclusive atmosphere. However, I recently faced one of my toughest trials: receiving the lowest educator evaluation I had ever encountered, despite my extensive experience as a K-12 English Language Arts teacher. This was more than just a statistic to me; it felt like a stinging betrayal, a stark contrast to the commitment and passion I brought to my classroom daily.

Though recognized as a highly effective veteran teacher and having played a crucial role in founding a successful charter school—an endeavor requiring intense teamwork and unwavering dedication—I found myself sidelined when it came to promotions. My qualifications were solid; I held school supervisor certifications and had nearly a decade of experience in that institution. Yet, I watched colleagues with less experience and lower evaluation scores leap into supervisory roles, which led to growing frustration beneath the surface.

It's challenging to summarize the whirlwind of experiences I faced throughout my career, particularly regarding my appearance and the biases that followed me. I vividly remember walking into the teacher's lounge one day and hearing snickers and whispers about my clothing choices. My wardrobe, a reflection of my personal style, was mocked by some of my colleagues who didn't understand it. They overlooked the hard work I put into teaching and instead viewed me through the narrow lens of stereotypes tied to my natural body shape.

Motivated by envy and a desire to undermine me, a few teachers went so far as to fabricate complaints to our supervisor, who happened to be of Turkish descent. The weight of their accusations was pressing. To appease this group and relieve mounting tension, I found myself swiping my credit card to purchase clothes over twice my regular size, all in an effort to fit into expectations that were never mine. I was determined to maintain my reputation as a highly effective teacher, and in some ways, I succeeded—until I took a bold step.

With hope in my heart, I applied to a school district more reflective of my ethnic background, that was located closer to my home—a predominantly Latinx community. It felt like a chance to break free from the constraints and judgments I had faced. However, when I encountered the school superintendent, a man who shared my ethnicity, I was blindsided by an evaluation that shattered my expectations. Receiving a score of 1 on a 1-4 scale in the Charlotte Danielson model was an unexpected blow, especially after years of hard work and dedication.

During our meeting, I couldn't shake the feeling that his feedback came from another universe. It was as though he was critiquing a fictional novel I had published on Amazon, discussing something entirely foreign to my reality. The disconnect between my genuine passion for teaching and his harsh assessment left me questioning everything: Did my accomplishments truly mean nothing? Was I to be judged solely by the fabric of my clothing and the color of my skin?

This experience—and many others like it—has taught me that biases can manifest in unexpected ways, and sometimes the people you hope to connect with the most can be the most critical. Ultimately, it has fueled my determination to advocate not only for my journey but also for the diverse voices in education that need to be heard and respected. This showed me that jealous has no bounds as a school superintendent Latinx descent evaluated ME, a Latina educational leader even worse than ALL other supervisor's individuals of other ethnicities; as all of the prior supervisors I've had prior to this year were predominantly of Turkish, Italian, Black or Caucasian ethnic descent, yet, they always provided a fairly accurate effective or highly effective overall teaching rating; truly aligning with my efforts and dedication to my profession. This means that the Latinx superintendent that evaluated me this year indicated "1's" which rated me as completely "unsatisfactory," on a scale of 1 to 4 in my second formal teaching evaluation for the academic year 204-2025.

On the same day of the evaluation, I reported a group of students in my classroom for misbehavior during instructional time, including talking back to me, throwing water and garbage on the floors of the classroom, and not adhering to the school's cell phone policy. A Latina school principal was present and witnessed the disorganization caused by these students, as well as my diligent efforts to restore order and keep them focused on their classwork. A few minutes later, I was informed by the male Latinx superintendent and the Latina principal that the group of students I had reported had made false complaints against me, mainly based on my physical appearance. I am a hardworking Latina with five college degrees, including one degree and two teaching credentials from the prestigious Rutgers University, New Brunswick, which is considered one of the best, if not the ultimate, college institution in the entire state of New Jersey. It's worth noting that even during my first year of teaching, I was evaluated as a highly effective teacher. I have never received such a low evaluation before, not even in my first year. Additionally, all of my supervisors in previous years encouraged me to embrace my leadership qualities and supported my growth as a leader.

I never imagined that just one year after obtaining my doctoral degree in educational administration from Rowan University, a respected research institution in New Jersey, I would receive such a terrible evaluation. This evaluation undermined all of my efforts in the teaching profession as well as the accomplishments I achieved at various universities, including, but not limited to, Rutgers University, New Brunswick, Middlesex College, Montclair State University, the Rutgers Center for Effective Teaching Practices, and Rowan University, where I graduated with high academic honors.

Before the incident that shook my professional journey, I had the privilege of working under a series of dedicated supervisors in the education field. Each of them strived diligently to ensure that evaluation scores were fair and accurate. Their unwavering commitment to excellence served as a powerful source of inspiration for me.

Their leadership not only ignited a deeper passion for teaching within me but also fueled my ambition to pursue advanced degrees. I fondly recall instances when many of my former supervisors recognized my potential and offered me promotions without requiring me to submit an application. Throughout my career, I have been actively recruited for various opportunities, including earning my master's degree in Educational Administration and pursuing my doctoral degree. For my doctoral program, the application fees were waived because the academic institutions felt honored to endorse me as an alumnus of my graduate school. My supervisors have consistently recognized and valued my leadership abilities in the workplace.

By the year 2024, I earned my doctoral degree, and now, in 2025, I anticipate that my career will flourish even further, building on the encouragement I received since the inception of my academic career.

However, the path was not without its challenges. I faced the insidious threat of microaggressions and invalidating remarks about my natural body shape, traits that I inherited from my parents and that I cannot change. In these moments of distress, I was grateful that my former supervisors stood by me. They chose not to engage with the negative commentary, refusing to allow false allegations to cloud my reputation or inflict emotional harm. Instead, they continued to extend opportunities for career advancement, recognizing my hard work and dedication regardless of the external noise. Their steadfast support has been a cornerstone of my resilience, and it reminds me of the profound impact that compassionate leadership can have in a challenging environment.

However, this academic year (2024-2025) in the workplace, in the vibrant corridors of a New Jersey school, a palpable tension brewed among a group of young girls of Latinx descent. This tension, it seemed, stemmed from a sense of jealousy towards a dedicated woman, a beacon of ambition and hard work in their midst and anger after being penalized for disrespectful behavior in the workplace. This group of students threatened me in my own classroom, several minutes after I had reported them to the administration team at the school; the security team and the school principal who is a Latina woman supported my efforts to penalize the poorly behaved scholars. However, the male school superintendent, whom is of Latinx ethnic descent did not seem too supportive as on the same day he had provided me an unsatisfactory teaching evaluation score, which undermined my efforts as a hardworking woman with a longstanding successful career trajectory in the state of New Jersey as a K-12 educator and student.

My journey through K-12 education, my role as a P-20 educator, and my unwavering commitment to earning five college degrees—all rooted in the very state I call home; New Jersey—stood as a testament to my perseverance and the heights one can reach through dedication.

Yet, instead of acquiring support, from a male Latinx school superintendent, after the group of female students were angry and retaliated because I reported their misbehavior; I found myself the target of hurtful stereotypes. I was even investigated for these false allegations by the department of children and families in the state of New Jersey, despite the noted fact that the students retaliated by generating false allegations after I reported their misbehavior. Rapidly afterwards, whispers filled the hallways as these young girls accused me of inappropriately "pointing my butt towards students" while teaching, a deeply offensive and unfounded allegation. This assertion felt like a calculated attempt to undermine the very legitimacy of my teaching certification, the cornerstone of my career, fueled solely by jealousy and misperceptions, merely based on my physical appearance, which is a factor beyond my control; and should be merely attributed to genetics-we look the way we look based on our ancestry, heritage or familial lineage.

Each incident, though just a fraction of the emotional turmoil I've endured, painted a stark picture of bias and envy that has influenced my work environment. With every disparaging comment, my efforts—a hard-working professional who has poured countless hours, energy, and financial resources into her passion—have been diminished. I've navigated these challenges without ever taking a sabbatical, fueled by my commitment to my students and my belief in the transformative power of education. Yet, despite these sacrifices, the shadows of stereotypes and envious glances continue to cast doubt on my path, urging me to rise above and remain steadfast in my mission.

It was disheartening to witness this disparity, where merit seemed to take a backseat to bias, reinforcing the notion that my identity as a Latina somehow diminished my achievements in the eyes of those making pivotal decisions. However, through this tangled web of experiences—each one a thread in the tapestry of my journey—I unearthed an unexpected source of strength. Each setback fueled my determination, igniting a fire within me that urged me to break down barriers and redefine my narrative.

Instead of allowing these challenges to hinder my aspirations, I chose to embrace them as learning opportunities. They compelled me to dig deep, fostering a resilience I didn't know existed within me. This newfound purpose crystallized into a profound realization: I needed to expand my horizons further and pursue a doctoral degree. I envisioned a future where I could amplify my voice and contribute to dismantling the biases that pervade our educational systems.

In this pursuit of higher education, I see not just a personal goal, but a mission to inspire and empower others who navigate similar challenges. My journey may be laden with hurdles, but it's also rich with invaluable lessons of perseverance and hope, underscoring the belief that dreams can be realized, even when the path is steep and winding. As I continue on this path, I am committed to transforming my experiences into a catalyst for change, paving the way for future generations of Latina entrepreneurs to rise and thrive against all odds.

As a proud Latina self-published author, teacher, and mentor, I've embarked on a multifaceted professional journey that has been both exhilarating and challenging. My role at Women into Networking (WIN), a vibrant women-owned business led by my dear friend Allegra Jackson, is a testament to my commitment to empowering others while navigating the complexities of my own path.

In the classroom, I passionately serve as an English Language Arts Teacher, where every lesson is an opportunity to inspire my students to find their voices. Beyond teaching, I embrace the role of a novice teacher mentor and departmental chair, guiding new educators as they embark on their own journeys. It's a position that should be filled with promise, yet despite my school supervisory certifications, I often find myself overlooked for advancement opportunities. Each missed opportunity, tinged with bias, serves as a reminder of the persistent challenges that women and people of color face in the professional landscape.

My entrepreneurial journey has been equally fraught with obstacles, as I navigate an arena that is often tinged with both gender and ethnic biases. Each step feels like a test, pushing the boundaries of my skills, creativity, and resilience. From launching my books to establishing connections within my community, I strive to carve out a space where my story can inspire others. It's a path less traveled, filled with both hurdles and triumphs, but through steadfast determination, I am committed to embracing the journey and paving the way for those who follow.

A moment that encapsulated the essence of my early experiences. I remember attending a networking event designed for entrepreneurs—an opportunity I seized with both excitement and anxiety. Upon entering the room, I was greeted by an overwhelmingly homogeneous group of individuals. As conversations began to unfold, I quickly became aware of the subtle, yet pervasive tone of bias. My presence as a Latina woman invoked a shift in dynamics; questions about my qualifications and capabilities seemed to linger unspoken in the air.

This scenario was not unique. Time and again, I encountered the implications of gender bias—my ideas questioned, my authority dismissed. It was as if the room became a microcosm of a broader societal mindset, perpetuating stereotypes that painted women, particularly women of color, as less competent or worthy of being taken seriously. Ethnic bias compounded these challenges. The assumption that I was there to provide translation services rather than to showcase my own business venture was a stark reminder of the barriers I faced. Yet, rather than shy away from these obstacles, I resolved to confront them head-on. I leaned into my cultural identity, recognizing that my heritage was not a hindrance but a source of strength. Each time I faced skepticism, I drew on the tenacity of my ancestors who had weathered their own storms, instilling within me a fierce determination to succeed.

These experiences ignited an intrinsic fire within me that impelled my journey toward higher education, personal excellence and sustained commitment to my own mental health and wellbeing because an empty canister is never able to flourish flowers around them, therefore, I ensure to take care of myself prior to preoccupying myself with the opinions of others, specially when they are not in alignment with my self perception.

I realized that to challenge the deeply rooted biases, I needed to arm myself with knowledge. Pursuing my doctoral degree became more than a personal aspiration; it transformed into a mission to empower other women who encountered similar hurdles, amid this I even became Dr. World Latina, to advocate for Latina rights particularly in the field of leadership; entrepreneurship and increasing the representation of women's managerial roles in all career fields (e.g: law enforcement, STEM, and business ownership).

My doctoral studies centered on the intersections of gender, ethnicity, and entrepreneurial success, and through research, I sought to uncover the systemic barriers that hinder women like me. During my doctoral journey, I met many incredible women who shared their stories of struggle and resilience. Each narrative reinforced my belief that we, as Latina entrepreneurs, are not alone. Together, we form a powerful network, lifting each other despite societal restraints. I learned about the importance of mentorship, community support, and advocacy within this space—essential elements to breaking down the glass ceiling that continues to loom over us.

The path toward entrepreneurship may be fraught with challenges, but it is also rich with triumphs. I stand today as a testament to the possibility of overcoming adversity, armed with my education and a network of inspiring women who refuse to accept the status quo. Each victory, whether large or small, is a step toward redefining perceptions and creating opportunities for future generations.

In conclusion, my journey as a Latina entrepreneur is an ongoing narrative of pushing past biases, both gendered and ethnic, and transforming those experiences into a source of empowerment. As I continue to advocate for equality and champion the voices of women in business, I remain dedicated to dismantling the barriers that hinder our progress. Together, we are breaking the glass ceiling—one story, one triumph at a time.

JOIN THE MOVEMENT!
#BAUW

Becoming An Unstoppable Woman
With She Rises Studios

She Rises Studios was founded by Hanna Olivas and Adriana Luna Carlos, the mother-daughter duo, in mid-2020 as they saw a need to help empower women worldwide. They are the podcast hosts of the *She Rises Studios Podcast* and Amazon best-selling authors and motivational speakers who travel the world. Hanna and Adriana are the movement creators of #BAUW - Becoming An Unstoppable Woman: The movement has been created to universally impact women of all ages, at whatever stage of life, to overcome insecurities, and adversities, and develop an unstoppable mindset. She Rises Studios educates, celebrates, and empowers women globally.

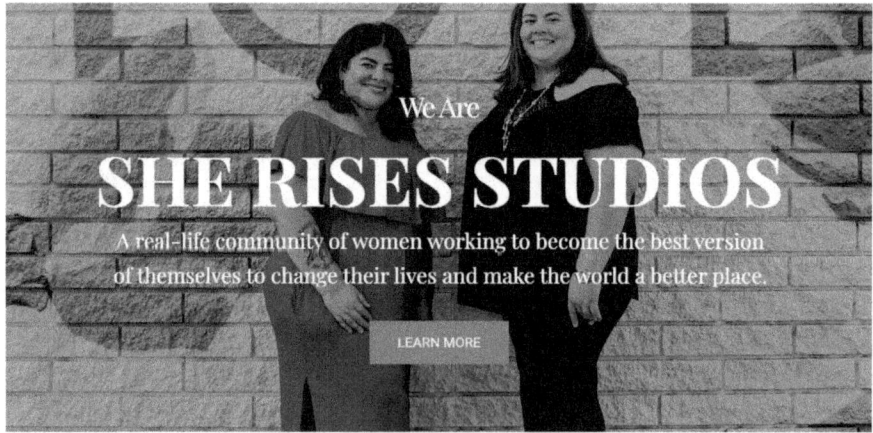

Looking to Join Us in our Next Anthology or Publish YOUR Own?

She Rises Studios Publishing offers full-service publishing, marketing, book tour, and campaign services. For more information, contact info@sherisesstudios.com

We are always looking for women who want to share their stories and expertise and feature their businesses on our podcasts, in our books, and in our magazines.

SEE WHAT WE DO

OUR PODCAST	OUR BOOKS	OUR SERVICES

Be featured in the Becoming An Unstoppable Woman magazine, published in 13 countries and sold in all major retailers. Get the visibility you need to LEVEL UP in your business!

Have your own TV show streamed across major platforms like Roku TV, Amazon Fire Stick, Apple TV and more!

Learn to leverage your expertise. Build your online presence and grow your audience with FENIX TV.
https://fenixtv.sherisesstudios.com/

Visit www.SheRisesStudios.com to see how YOU can join the #BAUW movement and help your community to achieve the UNSTOPPABLE mindset.

Have you checked out the *She Rises Studios Podcast?*

Find us on all MAJOR platforms: Spotify, IHeartRadio, Apple Podcasts, Google Podcasts, etc.

Looking to become a sponsor or build a partnership?

Email us at info@sherisesstudios.com

SHE RISES
S T U D I O S